Vocabu-Lit
Building Vocabulary Through Literature

Book K

Perfection Learning®

Acknowledgments

Excerpt from *Tracks* by Louise Erdrich, © 1988 by Louise Erdrich. Reprinted by permission of Henry Holt and Company.

Excerpt from *Locked Rooms and Open Doors: Diaries and Letters of Anne Morrow Lindbergh 1932–1935* by Anne Morrow Lindbergh. Copyright © 1974 by Anne Morrow Lindbergh. Reprinted by permission of Harcourt, Inc.

Excerpt from *In My Place* by Charlayne Hunter-Gault. Copyright © 1992 by Charlayne Hunter-Gault. Reprinted by permission of Farrar, Straus & Giroux, LLC.

Excerpt from *Africans in America* by Patricia Smith and Charles Johnson. Copyright © 1998 by WGBH Educational Foundation, with the exception of the fictional material by Charles Johnson. Fictional Material Copyright © 1998 by Charles Johnson. Reprinted by permission of Harcourt, Inc.

Perfection Learning®

Paperback ISBN-10: 0-7891-5657-1 ISBN-13: 978-0-7891-5657-0

26 27 PP 18 17

Table of Contents

Using the *Vocabu-Lit* Program

Vocabu-Lit is a unique vocabulary program. In format and approach, it differs in several ways from the usual vocabulary-building materials.

First, **Vocabu-Lit** contains examples of how the vocabulary words have been used by various writers and speakers. Reading the different passages not only will expose you to good writing but also will show you how vocabulary can become an effective writing tool.

Second, **Vocabu-Lit** does not ask you to learn a large number of words at one sitting. Instead, you work with just ten words at a time and are provided several experiences with those words. Each experience reinforces the previous one, helping you to master meaning.

Third, **Vocabu-Lit** takes advantage of the way you naturally acquire language by having you study words in context. Learning words through context aids you in two ways. First, it leads you to define a word more precisely. It also helps you develop an important reading skill: the ability to use clues from surrounding words and sentences to determine a word's meaning.

Reading the Passage

Each lesson begins with a selection from a book, essay, story, poem, or speech. You are encouraged to read straight through the selection without paying particular attention to the Master Words (the ten words in dark type). Your understanding of the general meaning of the passage should help you determine the definitions of the Master Words. Then you are advised to read the passage again, this time paying closer attention to the Master Words.

Self-Testing for Understanding

The first exercise is a self-test. It will help you identify the words that you have not yet mastered. Often you may think

you know a Master Word. But the meaning you know may differ from the meaning of the word as it is used in the passage. Or you may be unable to state the exact definition of a word. This exercise teaches you to look at a word in context and define its meaning more precisely.

To examine a word in context, you can study the surrounding words and sentences. For example, "He was **mendicant** because he had to beg." Using the context "because he had to beg," you may be able to tell that a mendicant is a beggar. Other times, opposite or contrasting terms may reveal the meaning: "He was far from poor; in fact, he was **affluent**." Obviously, in this context, **affluent** means "rich." Sometimes an unfamiliar word may be followed by examples that explain it, as in "Mrs. Murphy was a **hospitable** woman who warmly welcomed her son's friends." Key words such as **means, is, for example, in other words,** or **and so forth** may help determine a word's meaning.

Note: In some cases, the form of the Master Word in the self-test is not the same as in the passage. Generally, these changes were made to provide you with a more commonly used form of the word.

Writing Definitions

In the second exercise, you are asked to write definitions of the Master Words. The first part of the exercise asks that you define as many of the ten words as you can without using a dictionary. You should use context clues from the passage and any previous experience that you may have had with the words to write your definitions.

The second part of the exercise asks you to look up each word in a dictionary and copy an appropriate definition in the space provided. You may wish to compare this definition to your definition.

Note: The part of speech of the words as they will be used in the **exercises** is already indicated in the exercise. This may be different from the words' function in the passage, but you may still find it helpful to look for clues in the surrounding words or sentences.

Choosing Synonyms and Antonyms

This exercise asks you to pick a synonym and antonym for each Master Word. A synonym is a world that means **nearly the same** as another; an antonym is a word that means **nearly the opposite**.

Since you may not be familiar with all the words in the list of synonyms and antonyms, you may find it useful to keep a dictionary handy.

Note: There are no appropriate antonyms for some Master Words. In such cases, the antonym blank has been marked with an X. Also, a synonym or antonym may seem to match more than one Master Word in the exercise. Try to choose the word that is the best synonym or antonym for each Master Word.

Completing Analogies

In the fourth exercise, you are asked to complete word analogies using the Master Words. (An analogy is a comparison between two or more related things.) Again, you will be working with synonyms and antonyms (though different from those in the third exercise).

This exercise contains two types of analogies—words expressing **similar** relationships and words expressing **opposite** relationships. Look at the following example.

> day   :night   ::rich   : _____

The symbol : means "is to" and :: means

"as." Thus, the analogy could be read "Day is to night as rich is to _____."

The words **day** and **night** are opposites, or antonyms. So you should look for an antonym of **rich** in your list of Master Words. The Master Word **penniless** would be a correct response.

Fitting Words into Context

The next exercise includes ten sentences. You are to complete each sentence with the appropriate Master Word. Each sentence supplies clues to help you select the best answer. Thus, while testing your understanding of the new words, this exercise also provides practice for using the Master Words in context.

Playing with the Words

In the final exercise, you use the Master Words to solve a variety of puzzles. Traditional games such as acrostics, crosswords, and word spirals are offered. But there are also more unusual puzzles that challenge you to complete play associations and word fact tables, and to arrange words by degree. Another word game asks you to invent definitions for words that have been created by joining parts of the Master Words. You are even invited to write stories using some of your newly acquired vocabulary.

Reviewing Knowledge

There are three review lessons in every **Vocabu-Lit** (Lessons 12, 24, and 36). These lessons test your mastery of the vocabulary words from the previous eleven lessons by having you complete more sentences and analogies.

Read the following selection to get the general meaning. Read it a second time, paying special attention to the words in dark type. Notice how they are used in sentences. These are Master Words. These are the words you will be working with in this lesson.

From "The Story of an Eye-Witness"
by Jack London

Within an hour after the earthquake shock the smoke of San Francisco's burning was a **lurid** tower visible a hundred miles away. And for three days and nights this lurid tower swayed in the sky, reddening the sun, darkening the day, and filling the land with smoke.

On Wednesday morning at a quarter past five came the earthquake. A minute later the flames were leaping upward. In a dozen different quarters south of Market Street, in the working-class ghetto, and in the factories, fires started. There was no opposing the flames. There was no organization, no communication. All the **cunning** adjustments of a twentieth century city had been smashed by the earthquake. The streets were humped into ridges and depressions, and piled with the **debris** of fallen walls. The steel rails were twisted into **perpendicular** and horizontal angles. The telephone and telegraph systems were **disrupted.** And the great water-mains had burst. All the shrewd **contrivances** and safeguards of man had been thrown out of gear by thirty seconds' twitching of the earthcrust.

By Wednesday afternoon, inside of twelve hours, half the heart of the city was gone. At that time I watched the vast **conflagration** from out on the bay. It was dead calm. Not a flicker of wind stirred. Yet from every side wind was pouring in upon the city. East, west, north, and south, strong winds were blowing upon the doomed city. The heated air rising made an enormous suck. Thus did the fire of itself build its own **colossal** chimney through the atmosphere. . . .

Wednesday night saw the destruction of the very heart of the city. Dynamite was **lavishly** used . . . but there was no withstanding the onrush of the flames. Time and again successful stands were made by the fire-fighters, and every time the flames **flanked** around on either side, or came up from the rear and turned to defeat the hard-won victory.

EXERCISE 1

SELF-TEST: After reading the above selection, do the following. Look at the Master Words below. Underline the words that you think you know. Circle the words that you are less sure about. Draw a square around the words you don't recognize.

MASTER WORDS

colossal	disrupted
conflagration	flank
contrivance	lavishly
cunning	lurid
debris	perpendicular

Read the selection on the preceding page again, this time paying special attention to the ten Master Words. In the (a) spaces provided below, write down what you think is the meaning of the word. After you have attempted a definition for each word, look up the word in a dictionary. In the (b) spaces, copy the appropriate dictionary definition.

1. **colossal** (adj.)

   a. _Something big and exciting_

   b. _extremely large_

2. **conflagration** (n.)

   a. _____

   b. _an extensive fire which destroys a great deal of land or property_

3. **contrivance** (n.)

   a. _____

   b. _the use of skill to bring something about or create something_

4. **cunning** (adj.)

   a. _Good and smart_

   b. _having or showing skill in achieving one's ends by deceit or evasion_

5. **debris** (n.)

   a. _Trash and broken things_

   b. _scattered pieces of waste or remains_

6. **disrupted** (adj.)

   a. _delayed stopped_

   b. _interrupt (an event, activity, or process) by causing a disturbance or problem_

7. **flank** (v.)

   a. _To counter manuver_

   b. _the side of a persons or animals body between the ribs and the hip_

8. **lavishly** (adv.)

   a. _____

   b. _in a sumptuously rich, elaborate, or luxurios manner_

9. **lurid** (adj.)

   a. _____

   b. _very vivid in color, especially so as to create an unpleasantly harsh or unnatural effect_

10. **perpendicular** (adj.)

   a. _____

   b. _at an angle of 90° to a given line, plane, or surface_

Use the following list of synonyms and antonyms to fill in the blanks. Some words have no antonyms. In such cases, the antonym blanks have been marked with an X.

blaze	functioning	reconstruction	sparingly
crafty	horizontal	ruins	unsophisticated
device	luxuriously	sensational	vertical
diminutive	penetrate	skirt	wholesome
disturbed	prodigious		

	Synonyms	**Antonyms**
1. **colossal**	_prodigious_	_diminutive_
2. **conflagration**	_blaze_	X
3. **contrivance**	_crafty_	X
4. **cunning**	_sensational_	_unsophisticated_
5. **debris**	_ruins_	_reconstruction_
6. **disrupted**	_disturbed_	_functioning_
7. **flank**	_penetrate_	_device_
8. **lavishly**	_luxuriously_	_sparingly_
9. **lurid**	_skirt_	_wholesome_
10. **perpendicular**	_horizontal_	_vertical_

EXERCISE 4 ▮▮▮▮▮▮▮▮▮▮▮▮▮▮▮▮▮▮▮▮▮▮

Decide whether the first pair in the items below are synonyms or antonyms. Then choose the Master Word that shows a similar relation to the word(s) preceding the blank.

1. undermine	:support	::operating	:	_disrupted_
2. malicious	:good-natured	::cheaply	:	_contrivance_
3. adverse	:conflicting	::border	:	_perpendicular_
4. electorate	:voters	::wreckage	:	_debris_
5. implement	:accomplish	::upright	:	
6. partisan	:unbiased	::small	:	_colossal_
7. propriety	:blunder	::mild	:	
8. mandate	:order	::inferno	:	
9. skepticism	:belief	::crude	:	
10. impose	:burden	::gadget	:	

EXERCISE 5

The Master Words in this lesson are repeated below. From the Master Words, choose the appropriate word for the blank in each of the following sentences. Write the word in the numbered space provided at the right.

| colossal | contrivance | debris | flank | lurid |
| conflagration | cunning | disrupted | lavishly | perpendicular |

1. (A, An) ...?... swept London in 1666, reducing much of the city to rubble.

2. A wreck at the freeway entrance ...?... traffic.

3. The first battalion will ...?... the front lines and try to surprise the enemy.

4. Colorful accounts of sensational happenings carried in big city newspapers usually include many ...?... details.

5. If the center pole is ...?..., a tent will most likely remain upright.

6. ...?... quarterbacks mix running and passing plays.

7. The pyramids are (a, an) ...?... monument to the engineering skill of an early people.

8. After the bombing, ...?... covered a mile-wide area.

9. The Hollywood star entertained friends ...?... at an exclusive restaurant.

10. That ...?... on the carburetor helps control pollution.

1. _conflagration_
2. _disrupted_
3. _flank_
4. _lurid_
5. _perpendicular_
6. _cunning_
7. _colossal_
8. _debris_
9. _lavishly_
10. _contrivance_

EXERCISE 6

Order the words in each item from *least* to *most*. Use the abbreviations *L* for "least" and *M* for "most." Leave the line before the word of the middle degree blank. The first word provides a clue about how to arrange the words. See the example.

demanding: ___require   _M_ impel   _L_ suggest
(*Suggest* indicates the least demanding; *impel* indicates the most demanding.)

1. destructive:	_M_ conflagration	___ flames	_L_ spark
2. clever:	___ dull	_M_ cunning	_L_ useful
3. interrupted:	___ continued	_M_ disrupted	_L_ cancelled
4. shocking:	___ ordinary	_L_ spicy	_M_ lurid
5. big:	_L_ limitless	___ large	_M_ colossal
6. excessive:	_M_ lavishly	_L_ moderately	___ economically
7. upright:	___ slanted	_L_ horizontal	_M_ perpendicular
8. forward:	_L_ lead	_M_ flank	___ trail
9. complex:	___ utensil	_M_ contrivance	_L_ factory
10. crumbled:	___ rot	_L_ crack	_M_ debris

LESSON ONE   4

Read the following selection to get the general meaning. Read it a second time, paying special attention to the words in dark type. Notice how they are used in sentences. These are Master Words. These are the words you will be working with in this section.

from **Tracks**
by Louise Erdrich

Days passed before the town went looking for the men. Lily was a bachelor, after all, and Tor's wife had **suffered** a blow to the head that made her forgetful. Understandable. But what about Regina? That would always remain a question in people's minds. For she said nothing about her husband's **absence** to anyone. The whole town was **occupied** with digging out, in high relief because even though the Catholic **steeple** had been ripped off like a **peaked** cap and sent across five fields, those **huddled** in the cellar were unhurt. Walls had fallen, windows were **demolished**, but the stores were intact and so were the bankers and shop owners who had taken refuge in their safes or beneath their cash registers. It was a **fair-minded** disaster, no one could be said to have suffered much more than the next, except for Kozka's Meats.

When Pete and Fritzie came home, they found that the boards of the front building had been split to kindling, piled in a huge pyramid, and the shop equipment was blasted far and wide. Pete paced off the distance the iron bathtub had been flung, a hundred feet. The glass candy case went fifty, and landed without so much as a cracked pane. There were other surprises as well, for the back rooms where Fritzie and Pete lived were undisturbed. Fritzie said the dust still coated her china figures, and upon her kitchen table, in the ashtray, **perched** the last cigarette she'd put out in haste. She lit and finished it, looking through the window. From there, she could see that the old smokehouse Fleur had slept in was crushed to a reddish sand and the stockpens were completely torn apart, the rails stacked **helter-skelter**. Fritzie asked for Fleur. People shrugged. Then she asked about the others, and suddenly, the town understood that three men were missing.

EXERCISE 1

SELF-TEST: After reading the above selection, do the following. Look at the Master Words below. Underline the words that you think you know. Circle the words that you are less sure about. Draw a square around the words you don't recognize.

MASTER WORDS

absence	occupied
demolished	peaked
fair-minded	perched
helter-skelter	steeple
huddled	suffered

Read the selection on the preceding page again, this time paying special attention to the ten Master Words. In the (a) spaces provided below, write down what you think is the meaning of the word. After you have attempted a definition for each word, look up the word in a dictionary. In the (b) spaces, copy the appropriate dictionary definition.

1. **absence** (n.)

   a. _____

   b. _____

2. **demolished** (v.)

   a. _____

   b. _____

3. **fair-minded** (adj.)

   a. _____

   b. _____

4. **helter-skelter** (adv.)

   a. _____

   b. _____

5. **huddled** (v.)

   a. _____

   b. _____

6. **occupied** (v.)

   a. _____

   b. _____

7. **peaked** (adj.)

   a. _____

   b. _____

8. **perched** (v.)

   a. _____

   b. _____

9. **steeple** (n.)

   a. _____

   b. _____

10. **suffered** (v.)

   a. _____

   b. _____

EXERCISE 3

Use the following list of synonyms and antonyms to fill in the blanks. Some of the words have no antonyms. In such cases, the antonym blanks have been marked with an X.

avoided	crowded together	idled	presence	scattered
biased	destroyed	impartial	rested	spire
busied	flattened	nonattendance	restored	sustained
carefully	haphazardly	pointed		

	Synonyms	**Antonyms**
1. **suffered**	_____	_____
2. **absence**	_____	_____
3. **occupied**	_____	_____
4. **steeple**	_____	X
5. **peaked**	_____	_____
6. **huddled**	_____	_____
7. **demolished**	_____	_____
8. **fair-minded**	_____	_____
9. **perched**	_____	X
10. **helter-skelter**	_____	_____

EXERCISE 4

Decide whether the first pair in the items below are synonyms or antonyms. Then choose the Master Word that shows a similar relation to the word(s) preceding the blank.

1. deter	:encourage	::avoided	: _____
2. waste	:squander	::pointed	: _____
3. fragile	:sturdy	::carefully	: _____
4. evaluate	:judge	::busied	: _____
5. trash	:rubbish	::rested	: _____
6. permanent	:temporary	::biased	: _____
7. threat	:menace	::spire	: _____
8. commonplace	:exotic	::presence	: _____
9. grieve	:mourn	::crowded together	: _____
10. breakthrough	:impasse	::restored	: _____

LESSON TWO

The Master Words in this lesson are repeated below. From the Master Words, choose the appropriate word for the blank in each of the following sentences. Write the word in the numbered space provided at the right.

absence	fair-minded	huddled	peaked	steeple
demolished	helter-skelter	occupied	perched	suffered

1. They say ...?... makes the heart grow fonder, but it just made her lonely for her friend.

1. _____

2. The cardinal ...?... alone on the mailbox, enjoying the freedom of the sunshine and warm winds.

2. _____

3. Their things were scattered ...?... around the room, as though the storm had struck inside as well as outside.

3. _____

4. She ...?... their taunting in silence, knowing that her protests would only make things worse.

4. _____

5. Between the volcano's eruption and the mudslide that followed, the little town was quickly ...?...

5. _____

6. The judge was ...?... and promised to hear all sides of the story.

6. _____

7. She missed the turn because her mind was ...?... with thoughts of the challenges ahead.

7. _____

8. The children ...?... together under the bridge, staying close to keep each other warm.

8. _____

9. Colored sprinkles clung to the ...?... top of the ice cream cone.

9. _____

10. The bells ringing in the ...?... filled the valley with joyful sounds.

10. _____

EXERCISE 6 ███

To complete this puzzle, fill in the Master Word associated with each phrase. Then unscramble the circled letters to form another Master Word from this lesson.

1. What the sign on the airplane restroom might say:

   Ⓞ _ _ _ _ Ⓞ _ _

2. What a daredevil might climb up to get a good view of the countryside:

   _ _ _ _ _ Ⓞ _

3. If you had to listen to a long lecture about responsibility, you might feel you had

   Ⓞ _ _ _ _ _ _ _

4. Another word for chaotically or carelessly:

   Ⓞ _ _ _ _ _ - _ _ _ _ _ _

5. What the football team did while deciding their next play:

   _ _ _ Ⓞ _ _ _

6. What a wasp might have done on your pop can at the picnic:

   _ _ _ _ _ _ Ⓞ

7. How your head might look if you were wearing a wizard's hat:

   _ Ⓞ _ _ _ _

8. You might wish for your annoying little brother's

   _ _ _ Ⓞ _ _ _

9. What you hope your parents will be when you tell them you broke their antique vase by accident:

   _ _ _ _ - Ⓞ _ _ _ _

Now unscramble the scrambled Master Word and write it here: _____

Read the following selection to get the general meaning. Read it a second time, paying special attention to the words in dark type. Notice how they are used in sentences. These are Master Words. These are the words you will be working with in this lesson.

From a speech by Richard M. Nixon

This Nation cannot long continue to live with its conscience if millions of its own people are unable to get an adequate diet.

Even in purely practical terms there are compelling considerations requiring this challenge to be met.

A child ill-fed is dulled in curiosity, lower in **stamina, distracted** from learning. A worker ill-fed is less productive, more often absent from work. The mounting cost of medical care for diet-related illnesses, remedial education required to overcome diet-related slowness in school, institutionalization and loss of full productive **potential**—all of these place a heavy economic burden on a society as a whole.

And for many of us, and for me, as I know for many of you, this subject also **evokes** vivid personal memories. I grew up in the Great Depression. I shall never forget the hopelessness that I saw so **starkly etched** on so many faces—the silent gratitude of others lucky enough to enjoy three square meals a day, or sometimes even one. . . .

We have come a long way since then, but we still have a long way to go.

The question is: What will we do about it?

We begin with the troublesome complex of definitions and causes.

Experts can argue—and they do—and you will—about the **magnitude** of the problem: About how many are hungry, how many malnourished, and how severely they are malnourished. **Precise statistical** data remain **elusive** and often contradictory.

EXERCISE 1

SELF-TEST: After reading the above selection, do the following. Look at the Master Words below. Underline the words that you think you know. Circle the words that you are less sure about. Draw a square around the words you don't recognize.

MASTER WORDS

distracted	potential
elusive	precise
etched	stamina
evokes	starkly
magnitude	statistical

Read the selection on the preceding page again, this time paying special attention to the ten Master Words. In the (a) spaces provided below, write down what you think is the meaning of the word. After you have attempted a definition for each word, look up the word in a dictionary. In the (b) spaces, copy the appropriate dictionary definition.

1. **distracted** (adj.)

   a. _____

   b. _____

2. **elusive** (adj.)

   a. _____

   b. _____

3. **etched** (v.)

   a. _____

   b. _____

4. **evokes** (v.)

   a. _____

   b. _____

5. **magnitude** (n.)

   a. _____

   b. _____

6. **potential** (n.)

   a. _____

   b. _____

7. **precise** (adj.)

   a. _____

   b. _____

8. **stamina** (n.)

   a. _____

   b. _____

9. **starkly** (adv.)

   a. _____

   b. _____

10. **statistical** (adj.)

   a. _____

   b. _____

Use the following list of synonyms and antonyms to fill in the blanks. Some words have no antonyms. In such cases, the antonym blanks have been marked with an X.

capability	engraved	exact	inaccurate
diverted	engrossed	expunges	insignificance
elicits	enormousness	fatigue	nonfactual
embossed	evasive	harshly	numerical
endurance	evident	impossibility	softly

	Synonyms	**Antonyms**
1. **stamina**	_____	_____
2. **distracted**	_____	_____
3. **potential**	_____	_____
4. **evokes**	_____	_____
5. **starkly**	_____	_____
6. **etched**	_____	_____
7. **magnitude**	_____	_____
8. **precise**	_____	_____
9. **statistical**	_____	_____
10. **elusive**	_____	_____

Decide whether the first pair in the items below are synonyms or antonyms. Then choose the Master Word that shows a similar relation to the word(s) preceding the blank.

1. humanely	:charitably	::calls	:	_____
2. debased	:tainted	::mathematical	:	_____
3. impunity	:pardon	::drawn	:	_____
4. dupe	:con artist	::unimportance	:	_____
5. cowed	:supported	::weariness	:	_____
6. horde	:few	::fuzzily	:	_____
7. inculcate	:influence	::possibility	:	_____
8. degenerate	:depraved	::slippery	:	_____
9. laudable	:dishonorable	::absorbed	:	_____
10. enfeebled	:energized	::inexact	:	_____

The Master Words in this lesson are repeated below. From the Master Words, choose the appropriate word for the blank in each of the following sentences. Write the word in the numbered space provided at the right.

distracted	etched	magnitude	precise	starkly
elusive	evokes	potential	stamina	statistical

1. The driver was ...?... by the billboard and rammed into the car ahead.

    1. _____

2. The sight of my childhood home ...?... fond memories of simple, carefree days.

    2. _____

3. The computer does ...?... analyses in seconds that would take a mathematician months to complete.

    3. _____

4. A four-minute mile is common now, but a runner still requires ...?... to accomplish this feat.

    4. _____

5. The ...?... of the king's palace astonished the simple peasants.

    5. _____

6. His name was ...?... on the bronze trophy.

    6. _____

7. Halfbacks have to be ...?... to escape the charge of bigger men who have more strength.

    7. _____

8. Dead trees and the thin dark branches ...?... outline the wintry landscape.

    8. _____

9. He has ...?... as a scholar but does not like to study.

    9. _____

10. Atomic clocks allow us to make unbelievably ...?... measurements of time.

    10. _____

To complete the crossword, choose the Master Word associated with each word or phrase below. Begin each answer in the square having the same number as the clue.

1. not paying attention

2. evidence, numerically speaking

3. the vastness of space, for example

4. what a promising athlete has

5. staying power

6. measured to the exact millimeter

7. portrayed in grim black and white

8. scratched into glass

9. like a sneaky thief

10. recalls things past

LESSON 4

Read the following selection to get the general meaning. Read it a second time, paying special attention to the words in dark type. Notice how they are used in sentences. These are Master Words. These are the words you will be working with in this section.

from **Locked Rooms and Open Doors: Diaries and Letters of Anne Morrow Lindbergh, 1933–1935**

by Anne Morrow Lindbergh

Monday, February 27, 1933

It isn't that the **anniversary** is so terrible in itself. It is the **recall** of that **eternal baffling** mystery of death, the knife edge that one cannot understand—so fine, so sharp, so invisible, and so definite. The knife edge of "Yesterday I had him—today I have not." "A year ago I had him—soon I will not be able to say it any longer."

Yesterday, today, tomorrow—in the **clamor** of those three words are all the unbearables.

The **punctuation** of anniversaries is terrible, like the closing of doors, one after another between you and what you want to hold on to.

Somehow I feel as if this year that is over for me was just beginning its eternal **round**, like those cheap trick round-stories. How angry I was as a child when they would begin again: "It was a dark and stormy night and a **band** of robbers were sitting around the fire. The captain spoke up, 'Antonio, tell us a story,' and Antonio continued as follows: 'It was a dark and, etc.'"

To E. L. L. L.   Englewood, March 1st

Dear M.

I write to you tonight because I know you are thinking about the same thing. Perhaps we do very often. Your lovely, lovely roses, reminding me of your thoughts of little Charles. Not that I make, or that you make, an anniversary of this day but I did **dread** it in that—a year gone—it took me further away from him. But to feel your message and thoughts **counteracts** that feeling, as though to say: We both know that we will never forget him, that he will never be any further away.

Thank you, and my love.

EXERCISE 1

SELF-TEST: After reading the above selection, do the following. Look at the Master Words below. Underline the words that you think you know. Circle the words that you are less sure about. Draw a square around the words you don't recognize.

MASTER WORDS

anniversary	dread
baffling	eternal
band	punctuation
clamor	recall
counteracts	round

13

LESSON FOUR

Read the selection on the preceding page again, this time paying special attention to the ten Master Words. In the (a) spaces provided below, write down what you think is the meaning of the word. After you have attempted a definition for each word, look up the word in a dictionary. In the (b) spaces, copy the appropriate dictionary definition.

1. **anniversary** (n.)

   a. _____

   b. _____

2. **baffling** (adj.)

   a. _____

   b. _____

3. **band** (n.)

   a. _____

   b. _____

4. **clamor** (n.)

   a. _____

   b. _____

5. **counteracts** (v.)

   a. _____

   b. _____

6. **dread** (v.)

   a. _____

   b. _____

7. **eternal** (adj.)

   a. _____

   b. _____

8. **punctuation** (n.)

   a. _____

   b. _____

9. **recall** (n.)

   a. _____

   b. _____

10. **round** (n.)

    a. _____

    b. _____

Use the following list of synonyms and antonyms to fill in the blanks. Some of the words have no antonyms. In such cases, the antonym blanks have been marked with an X.

annual observance	cycle	everlasting	neutralizes	silence
augments	de-emphasis	forgetting	remembrance	temporary
clarifying	din	gang	shrink from	welcome
confusing	emphasis			

	Synonyms	**Antonyms**
1. **anniversary**	_____	X
2. **recall**	_____	_____
3. **eternal**	_____	_____
4. **baffling**	_____	_____
5. **clamor**	_____	_____
6. **punctuation**	_____	_____
7. **round**	_____	X
8. **band**	_____	X
9. **dread**	_____	_____
10. **counteracts**	_____	_____

Decide whether the first pair in the items below are synonyms or antonyms. Then choose the Master Word that shows a similar relation to the word(s) preceding the blank.

1. fellowship	:camaraderie	::endless	:	_____
2. meander	:careen	::silence	:	_____
3. shape	:forge	::annual observance	:	_____
4. resurgence	:reawakening	::repeating pattern	:	_____
5. prim	:staid	::group	:	_____
6. undermine	:support	::intensifies	:	_____
7. revered	:sacred	::fear	:	_____
8. agitated	:nonchalant	::understatement	:	_____
9. allow	:accede	::puzzling	:	_____
10. erudite	:scholarly	::recollection	:	_____

The Master Words in this lesson are repeated below. From the Master Words, choose the appropriate word for the blank in each of the following sentences. Write the word in the numbered space provided at the right.

anniversary	band	counteracts	eternal	recall
baffling	clamor	dread	punctuation	round

1. A friendly greeting often ...?... the effects of loneliness.

1. _____

2. Is there anything noisier than the ...?... in a school cafeteria at lunchtime?

2. _____

3. December 7 is always remembered as the ...?... of the attack on Pearl Harbor.

3. _____

4. Jason found it easy to take tests because with his photographic memory he could use his instant ...?... of information.

4. _____

5. Without pictures or illustrations, following the directions for wiring the stereo was a(n) ...?... experience.

5. _____

6. "I absolutely ...?... taking those final exams," Rasheeva declared.

6. _____

7. They were a ragged, unpromising ...?... of youths, but the coach vowed to make a team of them yet.

7. _____

8. On the tombstone were the words, "Peace and ...?... Rest."

8. _____

9. His application letter was riddled with poor ...?... .

9. _____

10. September came and another ...?... of classes were about to begin.

10. _____

This exercise compares groups of words according to their relative degree or intensity. Indicate their relative levels or degree or intensity by placing an *L* for "lowest," an *M* for "medium," or an *H* for "highest" in the appropriate blank. Master Words may be used in a different part of speech. The first word or phrase in each series gives you the standard for comparison. See the example below.

how hot:	__H__ scorching	__L__ warm	__M__ sultry

(*Warm* indicates the least heat, *sultry* a medium amount, and *scorching* the greatest amount of heat.)

1. how long-lasting:	_____ temporary	_____ momentary	_____ eternal
2. how much fear:	_____ dread	_____ apprehension	_____ confidence
3. how noisy:	_____ silence	_____ clamor	_____ buzz
4. how clear:	_____ baffling	_____ ambiguous	_____ self-explanatory
5. how supportive:	_____ allows	_____ enhances	_____ counteracts
6. how frequent:	_____ centennial	_____ anniversary	_____ bicentennial

Read the following selection to get the general meaning. Read it a second time, paying special attention to the words in dark type. Notice how they are used in sentences. These are Master Words. These are the words you will be working with in this lesson.

From **Treasure Island**
by Robert Louis Stevenson

From the side of the hill, which was here steep and stony, a **spout** of gravel was **dislodged,** and fell rattling and bounding through the trees. My eyes turned instinctively in that direction, and I saw a figure leap with great **rapidity** behind the trunk of a pine. What it was, whether bear or man or monkey, I could in no wise tell. It seemed dark and shaggy; more I knew not. But the terror of this new **apparition** brought me to a stand.

I was now, it seemed, cut off upon both sides; behind me the murderers, before me this **lurking nondescript.** And immediately I began to prefer the dangers that I knew to those I knew not. . . .

Instantly the figure reappeared, and, making a wide circuit, began to head me off. I was tired, at any rate; but had I been as fresh as when I rose, I could see it was in vain for me to contend in speed with such an **adversary.** From trunk to trunk the creature flitted like a deer, running manlike on two legs, but unlike any man that I had ever seen, stooping almost double as it ran. Yet a man it was, I could no longer be in doubt about that.

I began to recall what I had heard of cannibals. I was within an ace of calling for help. But the mere fact that he was a man, however wild, had somewhat **reassured** me, and my fear of Silver began to **revive** in proportion. I stood still, therefore, and cast about for some method of escape; and as I was so thinking, the recollection of my pistol flashed into my mind. As soon as I remembered I was not defenseless, courage glowed again in my heart; and I set my face **resolutely** for this man of the island, and walked briskly toward him.

EXERCISE 1

SELF-TEST: After reading the above selection, do the following. Look at the Master Words below. Underline the words that you think you know. Circle the words that you are less sure about. Draw a square around the words you don't recognize.

MASTER WORDS

adversary	**rapidity**
apparition	**reassure**
dislodge	**resolute**
lurk	**revive**
nondescript	**spout**

Read the selection on the preceding page again, this time paying special attention to the ten Master Words. In the (a) spaces provided below, write down what you think is the meaning of the word. After you have attempted a definition for each word, look up the word in a dictionary. In the (b) spaces, copy the appropriate dictionary definition.

1. **adversary** (n.)

    a. _____

    b. _____

2. **apparition** (n.)

    a. _____

    b. _____

3. **dislodge** (v.)

    a. _____

    b. _____

4. **lurk** (v.)

    a. _____

    b. _____

5. **nondescript** (adj.)

    a. _____

    b. _____

6. **rapidity** (n.)

    a. _____

    b. _____

7. **reassure** (v.)

    a. _____

    b. _____

8. **resolute** (adj.)

    a. _____

    b. _____

9. **revive** (v.)

    a. _____

    b. _____

10. **spout** (n.)

    a. _____

    b. _____

Use the following list of synonyms and antonyms to fill in the blanks. Some words have no antonyms. In such cases, the antonym blanks have been marked with an X.

ally	encourage	opponent	steadfast
describable	flaunt	phantom	stream
discourage	indefinable	plug	swiftness
displace	inertia	resuscitate	vacillating
embed	kill	skulk	

	Synonyms	**Antonyms**
1. **spout**	_____	_____
2. **dislodge**	_____	_____
3. **rapidity**	_____	_____
4. **apparition**	_____	X _____
5. **lurk**	_____	_____
6. **nondescript**	_____	_____
7. **adversary**	_____	_____
8. **reassure**	_____	_____
9. **revive**	_____	_____
10. **resolute**	_____	_____

EXERCISE 4 ▰▰▰▰▰▰▰▰▰▰▰▰▰▰▰▰▰▰▰▰▰▰▰▰▰▰▰▰▰▰▰▰

Decide whether the first pair in the items below are synonyms or antonyms. Then choose the Master Word that shows a similar relation to the word(s) preceding the blank.

1. adherent	:foe	::partner	: _____
2. tread	:walk	::renew	: _____
3. conceive	:dream up	::pipe	: _____
4. cogitation	:thought	::prowl	: _____
5. external	:exterior	::quickness	: _____
6. imagination	:reality	::indecisive	: _____
7. sensible	:foolish	::implant	: _____
8. exhort	:encourage	::ghost	: _____
9. adversity	:prosperity	::definable	: _____
10. previous	:following	::dishearten	: _____

The Master Words in this lesson are repeated below. From the Master Words, choose the appropriate word for the blank in each of the following sentences. Write the word in the numbered space provided at the right.

adversary	dislodge	nondescript	reassure	revive
apparition	lurk	rapidity	resolute	spout

1. He noted the ...?... of his heartbeat after exercise.

1. _____

2. Occasionally a hit results when we ...?... a record that was popular years ago.

2. _____

3. Ahab scanned the skies for the ...?... of the killer whale.

3. _____

4. It is not a winning practice to underestimate the strength of your ...?... .

4. _____

5. Tour guides claim that more than one ...?... stalks the castle's infamous corridors.

5. _____

6. Danger may ...?... in a dark alley.

6. _____

7. Once in office, the incumbent becomes difficult to ...?... .

7. _____

8. He was (a, an) ...?... fellow, dressed in an unremarkable suit of dull colors.

8. _____

9. If you ...?... people as they learn, they will tend to make faster progress with your encouragement.

9. _____

10. We are ...?... in our determination to hold this line, no matter what losses the enemy may inflict.

10. _____

Fill in the chart below with the Master Word that fits each set of clues. Part of speech refers to the word's usage in the lesson. Use a dictionary when necessary.

Number of Syllables	Part of Speech	Other Clues	Master Word
4	noun	someone you have a "beef" with	1. _____
3	adjective	not apt to change your mind	2. _____
2	verb	bring to life again	3. _____
2	verb	what you might do to a splinter	4. _____
4	noun	run with this	5. _____
3	adjective	not noteworthy	6. _____
1	noun	water may gush through this	7. _____
4	noun	meeting one might "spook" you	8. _____
3	verb	to give hope	9. _____
1	verb	what a cat on the prowl will do	10. _____

LESSON 6

Read the following selection to get the general meaning. Read it a second time, paying special attention to the words in dark type. Notice how they are used in sentences. These are Master Words. These are the words you will be working with in this section.

from **In My Place**
by Charlayne Hunter-Gault

On January 9, 1961, I walked onto the campus at the University of Georgia to begin **registering** for classes. Ordinarily, there would not have been anything unusual about such a **routine** exercise, except, in this instance, the **officials** at the university had been fighting for two and a half years to keep me out. I was not socially, intellectually, or **morally undesirable**. I was Black. And no Black student had ever been admitted to the University of Georgia in its 176-year history. Until the **landmark** *Brown v. Board of Education* decision that in 1954 declared separate but equal schools **unconstitutional**, the university was protected by law in its **exclusion** of people like me. In applying to the university, Hamilton Holmes and I were making one of the first major tests of the court's **ruling** in Georgia, and no one was sure just how hard it would be to challenge nearly two hundred years of exclusive white **privilege**. It would take us two and a half years of fighting our way through the system and the courts, but finally, with the help of the NAACP Legal Defense and Educational Fund, Inc., and with the support of our family and friends, we won the right that should have been ours all along.

EXERCISE 1

SELF-TEST: After reading the above selection, do the following. Look at the Master Words below. Underline the words that you think you know. Circle the words that you are less sure about. Draw a square around the words you don't recognize.

MASTER WORDS

exclusion	registering
landmark	routine
morally	ruling
officials	unconstitutional
privilege	undesirable

Read the selection on the preceding page again, this time paying special attention to the ten Master Words. In the (a) spaces provided below, write down what you think is the meaning of the word. After you have attempted a definition for each word, look up the word in a dictionary. In the (b) spaces, copy the appropriate dictionary definition.

1. **exclusion** (n.)

    a. _____

    b. _____

2. **landmark** (adj.)

    a. _____

    b. _____

3. **morally** (adv.)

    a. _____

    b. _____

4. **officials** (n.)

    a. _____

    b. _____

5. **privilege** (n.)

    a. _____

    b. _____

6. **registering** (v.)

    a. _____

    b. _____

7. **routine** (adj.)

    a. _____

    b. _____

8. **ruling** (n.)

    a. _____

    b. _____

9. **unconstitutional** (adj.)

    a. _____

    b. _____

10. **undesirable** (adj.)

    a. _____

    b. _____

Use the following list of synonyms and antonyms to fill in the blanks. Some of the words have no antonyms. In such cases, the antonym blanks have been marked with an X.

administrators	dropping out	illegal	milestone	prerogative
commonplace	enrolling	inclusion	objectionable	shutting out
decree	ethically	inconsequential	pleasing	unethically
disadvantage	exceptional	legal		

	Synonyms	**Antonyms**
1. **registering**	_____	_____
2. **routine**	_____	_____
3. **officials**	_____	X
4. **morally**	_____	_____
5. **undesirable**	_____	_____
6. **landmark**	_____	_____
7. **unconstitutional**	_____	_____
8. **exclusion**	_____	_____
9. **ruling**	_____	X
10. **privilege**	_____	_____

Decide whether the first pair in the items below are synonyms or antonyms. Then choose the Master Word that shows a similar relation to the word(s) preceding the blank.

1. sacred	:secular	::dropping out	: _____
2. praise	:kudos	::ordinary	: _____
3. biased	:impartial	::pleasing	: _____
4. tease	:taunt	::turning point	: _____
5. daydream	:reverie	::verdict	: _____
6. messenger	:courier	::advantage	: _____
7. uplifting	:humiliating	::inclusion	: _____
8. ecstatic	:dismal	::unethically	: _____
9. permissive	:lenient	::administrators	: _____
10. ardent	:apathetic	::legal	: _____

The Master Words in this lesson are repeated below. From the Master Words, choose the appropriate word for the blank in each of the following sentences. Write the word in the numbered space provided at the right.

| exclusion | morally | privilege | routine | unconstitutional |
| landmark | officials | registering | ruling | undesirable |

1. Many people think that driving a car is a right, but it is really a(n) ...?... granted by each state.

1. _____

2. It was the ...?... of the school board that the student would be suspended.

2. _____

3. Some clubs practice ...?... because they do not want certain people or types of people to be members.

3. _____

4. Most of the ...?... in the organization were appointed by the mayor.

4. _____

5. The Supreme Court listened to the case and decided that the law was ...?... .

5. _____

6. Rosa Park's decision to refuse to give up her seat on a Montgomery, Alabama, bus was a(n) ...?... in the Civil Rights movement.

6. _____

7. On school nights, her ...?... was to eat dinner, watch TV for an hour, and then finish her homework.

7. _____

8. He felt queasy and anxious, since public speaking was one of the most ...?... activities he would ever do.

8. _____

9. Their parents were proud that they had grown to be such ...?... upright human beings.

9. _____

10. They hated ...?... for classes because it took hours of standing in line.

10. _____

EXERCISE 6 ■■■

Use at least six of the Master Words in an original paragraph that tells or begins to tell a story. You may use the Master Words as different parts of speech to suit your story.

_____

_____

_____

_____

_____

_____

_____

Read the following selection to get the general meaning. Read it a second time, paying special attention to the words in dark type. Notice how they are used in sentences. These are Master Words. These are the words you will be working with in this section.

from **Africans in America: America's Journey Through Slavery**
by Charles Johnson and Patricia Smith

From the time she joined the Wheatley household, the young girl [Phillis] displayed a curiosity and intelligence far beyond her years. Embraced and **tutored** by the family, she quickly mastered geography, history, astronomy, and English and Latin literature. She began to write **classically** influenced poetry, rich with rhythm and detail and informed by a wisdom she was too young to possess.

Inevitably, Phillis became a curiosity outside the circle of home—clergymen, literati, and members of the socially **elite** visited to marvel at her **myriad** talents. **Prominent** physician Dr. Benjamin Rush insisted that her "singular genius and accomplishments are such as not only do honour to her sex, but to human nature." The **pampered** young slave girl was a miracle, a **voracious** learner with poetry as her pulse.

However, she remained frail and **prone** to ill health. To **bolster** her strength, doctors prescribed a London sojourn, which **coincidentally** would also promote the publication of the young woman's first book of poetry. The book was published in London because American publishers did not believe that a black person could have written it.

EXERCISE 1

SELF-TEST: After reading the above selection, do the following. Look at the Master Words below. Underline the words that you think you know. Circle the words that you are less sure about. Draw a square around the words you don't recognize.

MASTER WORDS

bolster	pampered
classically	prominent
coincidentally	prone
elite	tutored
myriad	voracious

Read the selection on the preceding page again, this time paying special attention to the ten Master Words. In the (a) spaces provided below, write down what you think is the meaning of the word. After you have attempted a definition for each word, look up the word in a dictionary. In the (b) spaces, copy the appropriate dictionary definition.

1. **bolster** (v.)

    a. _____

    b. _____

2. **classically** (adv.)

    a. _____

    b. _____

3. **coincidentally** (adv.)

    a. _____

    b. _____

4. **elite** (n.)

    a. _____

    b. _____

5. **myriad** (adj.)

    a. _____

    b. _____

6. **pampered** (adj.)

    a. _____

    b. _____

7. **prominent** (adj.)

    a. _____

    b. _____

8. **prone** (adj.)

    a. _____

    b. _____

9. **tutored** (v.)

    a. _____

    b. _____

10. **voracious** (adj.)

    a. _____

    b. _____

Use the following list of synonyms and antonyms to fill in the blanks. Some of the words have no antonyms. In such cases, the antonym blanks have been marked with an X.

aristocracy	formally	neglected	satiated	undermine
atypically	inclined	obscure	simultaneously	well-known
disinclined	instructed	ravenous	spoiled	
few	many	reinforce	the masses	

	Synonyms	**Antonyms**
1. **tutored**	_____	X
2. **classically**	_____	_____
3. **elite**	_____	_____
4. **myriad**	_____	_____
5. **prominent**	_____	_____
6. **pampered**	_____	_____
7. **voracious**	_____	_____
8. **prone**	_____	_____
9. **bolster**	_____	_____
10. **coincidentally**	_____	X

Decide whether the first pair in the items below are synonyms or antonyms. Then choose the Master Word that shows a similar relation to the word(s) preceding the blank.

1. vigilant	:watchful	::concurrently	: _____
2. petition	:appeal	::disposed	: _____
3. adept	:adroit	::traditionally	: _____
4. contiguous	:adjoining	::taught	: _____
5. ripple	:undulate	::indulged	: _____
6. chronic	:acute	::the masses	: _____
7. lethargic	:sprightly	::unknown	: _____
8. moribund	:dying	::insatiable	: _____
9. sparse	:teeming	::undermine	: _____
10. conscientious	:wanton	::meager	: _____

The Master Words in this lesson are repeated below. From the Master Words, choose the appropriate word for the blank in each of the following sentences. Write the word in the numbered space provided at the right.

| bolster | coincidentally | myriad | prominent | tutored |
| classically | elite | pampered | prone | voracious |

1. The doctor decided to give the patient another vaccination in order to ...?... his immune system.

1. _____

2. Casey, a Dalmatian dog, ...?... died at the same moment its owner did.

2. _____

3. His ...?... inspired musical compositions improved with every attempt.

3. _____

4. Maple trees make fine shade trees, but their brittle wood makes them ...?... to broken limbs and branches.

4. _____

5. Her parents decided she should be ...?... at home while she recovered from her illness so she could keep up with her classes.

5. _____

6. She dressed and acted as though she were one of the cultured ...?..., though no one knew her outside of her little town.

6. _____

7. We were honored to have such a ...?... writer come and speak to our class.

7. _____

8. Even though the puppy chewed furniture, wet the rug, and whined throughout the night, its ...?... charms endeared itself to the owners.

8. _____

9. First a massage, then a sauna, and then a complete facial made for a ...?... day of luxury.

9. _____

10. The ...?... grasshoppers stripped the grain off the stalks in the field in no time at all, and went on their way to find more.

10. _____

Fill in the chart below with the Master Word that fits each set of clues. Part of speech refers to the way the word is used in this lesson. Use a dictionary when necessary.

Number of Syllables	Part of Speech	Other Clues	Master Word
3	Adjective	How you feel when you don't eat all day.	1. _____
2	Noun	You might dislike people who consider themselves part of this.	2. _____
3	Adjective	A nose, ears, or a famous person can be this.	3. _____
2	Adjective	Some people think grandchildren are treated this way by grandparents.	4. _____
4	Adverb	The same as a formal, typical way of learning.	5. _____
3	Adjective	Kinds of goods you might see in a bazaar; rhymes with "period."	6. _____
2	Verb	Taught by someone more knowledgeable.	7. _____

Read the following selection to get the general meaning. Read it a second time, paying special attention to the words in dark type. Notice how they are used in sentences. These are Master Words. These are the words you will be working with in this lesson.

From "The Sculptor's Funeral"
by Willa Cather

A group of the townspeople stood on the station siding of a little Kansas town, awaiting the coming of the night train, which was already twenty minutes overdue. The snow had fallen thick over everything; in the pale starlight the line of bluffs across the wide, white meadows south of the town made soft, smoke-coloured curves against the clear sky. The men on the siding stood first on one foot and then on the other, their hands **thrust** deep into their trousers pockets, their overcoats open, their shoulders screwed up with the cold; and they glanced from time to time toward the southeast, where the railroad track wound along the river shore. They **conversed** in low tones and moved about restlessly, seeming uncertain as to what was expected of them. There was but one of the company who looked as though he knew exactly why he was there, and he kept **conspicuously** apart, walking to the far end of the platform, returning to the station door, then pacing up the track again, his chin sunk in the high collar of his overcoat, his **burly** shoulders drooping forward, his **gait** heavy and **dogged.** Presently he was approached by a tall, spare, **grizzled** man clad in a faded Grand Army suit, who **shuffled** out from the group and advanced with a certain **deference, craning** his neck forward until his back made the angle of a jack-knife three-quarters open.

"I reckon she's a-goin' to be pretty late agin tonight, Jim," he remarked in a squeaky falsetto. "S'pose it's the snow?"

"I don't know," responded the other man with a shade of annoyance, speaking from out an astonishing cataract of red beard.

EXERCISE 1

SELF-TEST: After reading the above selection, do the following. Look at the Master Words below. Underline the words that you think you know. Circle the words that you are less sure about. Draw a square around the words you don't recognize.

MASTER WORDS

burly	dogged
conspicuous	gait
converse	grizzled
crane	shuffle
deference	thrust

Read the selection on the preceding page again, this time paying special attention to the ten Master Words. In the (a) spaces provided below, write down what you think is the meaning of the word. After you have attempted a definition for each word, look up the word in a dictionary. In the (b) spaces, copy the appropriate dictionary definition.

1. **burly** (adj.)

   a. _____

   b. _____

2. **conspicuous** (adj.)

   a. _____

   b. _____

3. **converse** (v.)

   a. _____

   b. _____

4. **crane** (v.)

   a. _____

   b. _____

5. **deference** (n.)

   a. _____

   b. _____

6. **dogged** (adj.)

   a. _____

   b. _____

7. **gait** (n.)

   a. _____

   b. _____

8. **grizzled** (adj.)

   a. _____

   b. _____

9. **shuffle** (v.)

   a. _____

   b. _____

10. **thrust** (v.)

   a. _____

   b. _____

Use the following list of synonyms and antonyms to fill in the blanks. Some words have no antonyms. In such cases, the antonym blanks have been marked with an X.

consideration	husky	retract	suppress
contempt	obscure	shove	talk
determined	pace	stance	wavering
drag	prominent	stretch	withdraw
gray	puny	stride	

	Synonyms	**Antonyms**
1. **thrust**	_____	_____
2. **converse**	_____	_____
3. **conspicuous**	_____	_____
4. **burly**	_____	_____
5. **gait**	_____	_____
6. **dogged**	_____	_____
7. **grizzled**	_____	X
8. **shuffle**	_____	_____
9. **deference**	_____	_____
10. **crane**	_____	_____

Decide whether the first pair in the items below are synonyms or antonyms. Then choose the Master Word that shows a similar relation to the word(s) preceding the blank.

1. exclude	:accept	::frail	:	_____
2. hamlet	:village	::hobble	:	_____
3. isolate	:unite	::pull back	:	_____
4. perfunctorily	:automatically	::regard	:	_____
5. clamber	:scramble	::step	:	_____
6. escort	:protection	::extend	:	_____
7. incline	:tend	::discuss	:	_____
8. sheer	:swerve	::silvery	:	_____
9. considerable	:scarce	::undecided	:	_____
10. tardily	:early	::unnoticeable	:	_____

The Master Words in this lesson are repeated below. From the Master Words, choose the appropriate word for the blank in each of the following sentences. Write the word in the numbered space provided at the right.

burly	converse	deference	gait	shuffle
conspicuous	crane	dogged	grizzled	thrust

1. An old miner with (a, an) ...?... beard stumbled into the saloon.

1. _____

2. The children ...?... their necks to peek out the window whenever a fire truck passes.

2. _____

3. He walked to the lecture platform at a brisk ...?..., carrying his speech notes and a small medal.

3. _____

4. The crowd saluted to show ...?... to the flag.

4. _____

5. A neon jacket will make you ...?... in traffic when you ride your bicycle.

5. _____

6. The ...?... tackle stormed across the line and laid the quarterback low.

6. _____

7. Despite his ...?... insistence that he was innocent, the jury announced a guilty verdict.

7. _____

8. The librarian hushed us, cautioning that we should only ...?... in low tones.

8. _____

9. Each morning, tapping his cane along the walk, the little old man would ...?... down to the post office for the mail.

9. _____

10. Macomber ...?... the spear into the side of the great beast.

10. _____

The invented words below are formed from parts of different Master Words from this lesson. Create a definition and indicate the part of speech for each word. The first one is done for you.

deferverse   *(v.) to converse in a highly respectful and courteous manner* _____

conspicuverse _____

cranethrust   _____

doggedgait   _____

Now invent your own words by combining parts of the Master Words. Create a definition for each, and indicate the word's part of speech. (You may reuse any of the word parts above in new combinations.)

1. _____   _____

2. _____   _____

LESSON 9

Read the following selection to get the general meaning. Read it a second time, paying special attention to the words in dark type. Notice how they are used in sentences. These are Master Words. These are the words you will be working with in this lesson.

From **The Oregon Trail**
by Francis Parkman

The rifle of Henry Chatillon was necessary for the **subsistence** of the party in my absence; so I called Raymond and ordered him to prepare to set out with me. Raymond rolled his eyes vacantly about, but at length, having succeeded in **grappling** with the idea, he withdrew to his bed under the cart. He was a heavy-moulded fellow, with a broad face, expressing **impenetrable** stupidity and entire self-confidence. As for his good qualities, he had a sort of stubborn **fidelity,** an **insensibility** to danger and a kind of instinct or **sagacity,** which sometimes led him right where better heads than his were at a loss. Besides this, he knew very well how to handle a rifle and picket a horse.

Through the following day the sun glared down upon us with a pitiless, penetrating heat. The distant blue prairie seemed **quivering** under it. The lodge of our Indian associates **parched** in the burning rays, and our rifles, as they leaned against the tree, were too hot for the touch. There was a dead silence through our camp, broken only by the hum of gnats and mosquitoes. The men, resting their foreheads on their arms, were sleeping under the cart. The Indians kept close within their lodge, except the newly-married pair, who were seated together under an awning of buffalo-robes, and the old **conjurer,** who, with his hard, **emaciated** face and gaunt ribs, was perched aloft.

EXERCISE 1

SELF-TEST: After reading the above selection, do the following. Look at the Master Words below. Underline the words that you think you know. Circle the words that you are less sure about. Draw a square around the words you don't recognize.

MASTER WORDS

conjurer	insensibility
emaciated	parch
fidelity	quiver
grapple	sagacity
impenetrable	subsistence

---

33   LESSON NINE

Read the selection on the preceding page again, this time paying special attention to the ten Master Words. In the (a) spaces provided below, write down what you think is the meaning of the word. After you have attempted a definition for each word, look up the word in a dictionary. In the (b) spaces, copy the appropriate dictionary definition.

1. **conjurer** (n.)

    a. _____

    b. _____

2. **emaciated** (adj.)

    a. _____

    b. _____

3. **fidelity** (n.)

    a. _____

    b. _____

4. **grapple** (v.)

    a. _____

    b. _____

5. **impenetrable** (adj.)

    a. _____

    b. _____

6. **insensibility** (n.)

    a. _____

    b. _____

7. **parch** (v.)

    a. _____

    b. _____

8. **quiver** (v.)

    a. _____

    b. _____

9. **sagacity** (n.)

    a. _____

    b. _____

10. **subsistence** (n.)

    a. _____

    b. _____

Use the following list of synonyms and antonyms to fill in the blanks. Some words have no antonyms. In such cases, the antonym blanks have been marked with an X.

allegiance	enfeebled	moisten	steady
callousness	exposed	scientist	strengthened
consciousness	impervious	scorch	stupidity
disloyalty	magician	shiver	wisdom
disregard	maintenance	starvation	wrestle

	Synonyms	**Antonyms**
1. **subsistence**	_____	_____
2. **grapple**	_____	_____
3. **impenetrable**	_____	_____
4. **fidelity**	_____	_____
5. **insensibility**	_____	_____
6. **sagacity**	_____	_____
7. **quiver**	_____	_____
8. **parch**	_____	_____
9. **conjurer**	_____	_____
10. **emaciated**	_____	_____

Decide whether the first pair in the items below are synonyms or antonyms. Then choose the Master Word that shows a similar relation to the word(s) preceding the blank.

1. burly	:weak	::faithlessness	:	_____
2. shuffle	:limp	::tremble	:	_____
3. thrust	:shove	::inaccessible	:	_____
4. gait	:pace	::sorcerer	:	_____
5. deference	:disrespect	::dampen	:	_____
6. crane	:stretch	::struggle	:	_____
7. dogged	:uncertain	::foolishness	:	_____
8. converse	:speak	::weak	:	_____
9. conspicuous	:unclear	::awareness	:	_____
10. grizzled	:gray	::existence	:	_____

The Master Words in this lesson are repeated below. From the Master Words, choose the appropriate word for the blank in each of the following sentences. Write the word in the numbered space provided at the right.

conjurer	fidelity	impenetrable	parch	sagacity
emaciated	grapple	insensibility	quiver	subsistence

1. I was shocked at his ...?... to the problems of others.   1. _____

2. The band of Sherwood Forest pledged ...?... to Robin Hood.   2. _____

3. The food bank needs donations to provide ...?... for the homeless.   3. _____

4. Supreme Court justices are supposed to have a special kind of ...?... that qualifies them to hand down justice.   4. _____

5. In August, the sun will ...?... the earth and clouds will gather, but no rain will fall.   5. _____

6. Movies with a monster or two are designed to make you ...?... .   6. _____

7. Becky lunged at the murderer and began to ...?... with him for the gun.   7. _____

8. Some people used to believe that only a witch or ...?... could swim.   8. _____

9. Even when attacked by battering rams and slings, the fortress proved ...?... .   9. _____

10. The religious zealot believed his ...?... body symbolized a pure soul.   10. _____

Write the Master Word that is associated with each word group below. Then list three things that might be associated with the review word that follows.

1. drought, sunburn, desert   _____

2. owl, Solomon, judge   _____

3. friends, promises, loyalty   _____

4. voice, nerves, lip   _____

5. secret code, fortress, bulletproof vest   _____

6. wrestlers, problem, conscience   _____

7. wand, Merlin, trick cards   _____

8. necessities, living, basics   _____

9. crash diet, famine, disease   _____

10. sleepwalking, knock-out, zombie   _____

Review word: dogged (Lesson 8)

_____   _____   _____

LESSON 10

Read the following selection to get the general meaning. Read it a second time, paying special attention to the words in dark type. Notice how they are used in sentences. These are Master Words. These are the words you will be working with in this lesson.

From **Street Life in New York**
by Horatio Alger

Among the down-town boot-blacks was one hailing from the Five Points,—a stout, red-haired, freckled-faced boy of fourteen, bearing the name of Micky Maguire. This boy, by his boldness and recklessness, as well as by his personal strength, which was considerable, had acquired an ascendency among his fellow professionals, and had a gang of subservient followers, whom he led on to acts of ruffianism, not unfrequently terminating in a month or two at Blackwell's Island. . . .

Now Micky was proud of his strength, and of the position of leader which it had secured him. Moreover he was democratic in his tastes, and had a jealous hatred of those who wore good clothes and kept their faces clean. He called it putting on airs, and resented the **implied superiority.** If he had been fifteen years older, and had a trifle more education, he would have interested himself in politics, and been **prominent** at ward meetings, and a terror to respectable voters on election day. As it was, he contented himself with being the leader of a gang of young **ruffians,** over whom he **wielded** a **despotic** power.

Now it is only justice to Dick to say that, so far as wearing good clothes was concerned, he had never hitherto offended the eyes of Micky Maguire. Indeed, they generally looked as if they patronized the same clothing establishment. On this particular morning it chanced that Micky had not been very fortunate in a business way, and, as a natural consequence, his temper, never very **amiable,** was somewhat **ruffled** by the fact. He had had a very **frugal** breakfast,—not because he felt **abstemious,** but owing to the low state of his finances.

EXERCISE 1

SELF-TEST: After reading the above selection, do the following. Look at the Master Words below. Underline the words that you think you know. Circle the words that you are less sure about. Draw a square around the words you don't recognize.

MASTER WORDS

abstemious	prominent
amiable	ruffian
despotic	ruffled
frugal	superiority
imply	wield

Read the selection on the preceding page again, this time paying special attention to the ten Master Words. In the (a) spaces provided below, write down what you think is the meaning of the word. After you have attempted a definition for each word, look up the word in a dictionary. In the (b) spaces, copy the appropriate dictionary definition.

1. **abstemious** (adj.)

   a. _____

   b. _____

2. **amiable** (adj.)

   a. _____

   b. _____

3. **despotic** (adj.)

   a. _____

   b. _____

4. **frugal** (adj.)

   a. _____

   b. _____

5. **imply** (v.)

   a. _____

   b. _____

6. **prominent** (adj.)

   a. _____

   b. _____

7. **ruffian** (n.)

   a. _____

   b. _____

8. **ruffled** (adj.)

   a. _____

   b. _____

9. **superiority** (n.)

   a. _____

   b. _____

10. **wield** (v.)

   a. _____

   b. _____

Use the following list of synonyms and antonyms to fill in the blanks. Some words have no antonyms. In such cases, the antonym blanks have been marked with an X.

assert	friendly	rowdy	supremacy
democratic	hostile	self-indulgent	temperate
disturbed	humbleness	socialite	thrifty
eminent	manipulate	soothed	tyrannical
extravagant	obscure	suggest	

	Synonyms	**Antonyms**
1. **imply**	_____	_____
2. **ruffled**	_____	_____
3. **prominent**	_____	_____
4. **ruffian**	_____	_____
5. **wield**	_____	X _____
6. **despotic**	_____	_____
7. **superiority**	_____	_____
8. **amiable**	_____	_____
9. **frugal**	_____	_____
10. **abstemious**	_____	_____

Decide whether the first pair in the items below are synonyms or antonyms. Then choose the Master Word that shows a similar relation to the word(s) preceding the blank.

1. quiver	:shake	::bully	: _____
2. fidelity	:deceit	::wasteful	: _____
3. impenetrable	:unprotected	::calmed	: _____
4. parch	:soak	::unfriendly	: _____
5. conjurer	:magician	::use	: _____
6. subsistence	:survival	::iron-handed	: _____
7. grapple	:tackle	::hint	: _____
8. emaciated	:wasted	::self-controlled	: _____
9. sagacity	:dullness	::unnoticed	: _____
10. insensibility	:sensitivity	::inferiority	: _____

The Master Words in this lesson are repeated below. From the Master Words, choose the appropriate word for the blank in each of the following sentences. Write the word in the numbered space provided at the right.

| abstemious | despotic | imply | ruffian | superiority |
| amiable | frugal | prominent | ruffled | wield |

1. The teacher seemed to ...?... that someone in the room was not telling the truth but didn't accuse anyone directly.

1. _____

2. (A, An) ...?... dieter who shuns rich food is likely to lose weight.

2. _____

3. Hitler's crusade was based on a claim of Aryan ...?... over the rest of the world.

3. _____

4. He was (a, an) ...?... fellow, always smiling and with a good word for everybody.

4. _____

5. Johnson was (a, an) ...?... member of the After Dinner Club and widely known in the state.

5. _____

6. The new company president seemed slightly ...?... when the meeting did not go well.

6. _____

7. You could always count on our student council president to ...?... his influence in a positive way.

7. _____

8. The jogger was assaulted by (a, an) ...?... in Greenwood Park.

8. _____

9. The people rebelled against the harsh, ...?... leader.

9. _____

10. Because taxes had been cut, the school was forced to operate on (a, an) ...?... budget.

10. _____

Order the words in each item from *least* to *most*. Use the abbreviations *L* for "least" and *M* for "most." Leave the line before the word of the middle degree blank. The first word provides a clue about how to arrange the words. See the example.

lively: __L__weary   __M__hyperactive   ____energetic
(*Weary* indicates the least lively; *hyperactive* indicates the most lively.)

1. assertive:	____withhold	____declare	____imply
2. restrained:	____gluttonous	____fasting	____abstemious
3. angered:	____furious	____ruffled	____bothered
4. warm:	____jolly	____amiable	____polite
5. stingy:	____generous	____frugal	____miserly
6. criminal:	____prankster	____ruffian	____terrorist
7. hidden:	____prominent	____concealed	____half-visible
8. excellent:	____efficiency	____superiority	____adequacy
9. restrictive:	____despotic	____regulating	____domineering
10. control:	____wield	____handle	____observe

Read the following selection to get the general meaning. Read it a second time, paying special attention to the words in dark type. Notice how they are used in sentences. These are Master Words. These are the words you will be working with in this lesson.

From **Little Dorrit**
by Charles Dickens

It was a Sunday evening in London, gloomy, **close,** and stale. Maddening church bells of all degrees of **dissonance,** sharp and flat, cracked and clear, fast and slow, made the brick-and-mortar echoes hideous. **Melancholy** streets, in a **penitential garb** of soot, **steeped** the souls of the people who were condemned to look at them out of windows, in **dire despondency.** In every thoroughfare, up almost every alley, and down almost every turning, some doleful bell was throbbing, jerking, tolling, as if the Plague were in the city and the dead-carts were going round. Everything was bolted and barred that could by possibility furnish relief to an overworked people. No pictures, no unfamiliar animals, no rare plants or flowers, no natural or artificial wonders of the ancient world—all **taboo** with that enlightened strictness, that the ugly South Sea gods in the British Museum might have supposed themselves at home again. Nothing to see but streets, streets, streets. Nothing to breathe but streets, streets, streets. Nothing to change the brooding mind, or raise it up. Nothing for the **spent** toiler to do, but to compare the monotony of his seventh day with the monotony of his six days, think what a weary life he led, and make the best of it—or the worst, according to the probabilities.

EXERCISE 1

SELF-TEST: After reading the above selection, do the following. Look at the Master Words below. Underline the words that you think you know. Circle the words that you are less sure about. Draw a square around the words you don't recognize.

MASTER WORDS

close	melancholy
despondency	penitential
dire	spent
dissonance	steep
garb	taboo

Read the selection on the preceding page again, this time paying special attention to the ten Master Words. In the (a) spaces provided below, write down what you think is the meaning of the word. After you have attempted a definition for each word, look up the word in a dictionary. In the (b) spaces, copy the appropriate dictionary definition.

1. **close** (adj.)

   a. _____

   b. _____

2. **despondency** (n.)

   a. _____

   b. _____

3. **dire** (adj.)

   a. _____

   b. _____

4. **dissonance** (n.)

   a. _____

   b. _____

5. **garb** (n.)

   a. _____

   b. _____

6. **melancholy** (adj.)

   a. _____

   b. _____

7. **penitential** (adj.)

   a. _____

   b. _____

8. **spent** (adj.)

   a. _____

   b. _____

9. **steep** (v.)

   a. _____

   b. _____

10. **taboo** (adj.)

    a. _____

    b. _____

Use the following list of synonyms and antonyms to fill in the blanks. Some words have no antonyms. In such cases, the antonym blanks have been marked with an X.

apparel	depression	forbidden	sanctioned
blue	discord	fresh	saturate
cheerful	dry out	harmony	stuffy
contrite	elation	invigorated	unimportant
critical	exhausted	remorseless	

	Synonyms	**Antonyms**
1. **close**	_____	_____
2. **dissonance**	_____	_____
3. **melancholy**	_____	_____
4. **penitential**	_____	_____
5. **garb**	_____	X _____
6. **steep**	_____	_____
7. **dire**	_____	_____
8. **despondency**	_____	_____
9. **taboo**	_____	_____
10. **spent**	_____	_____

Decide whether the first pair in the items below are synonyms or antonyms. Then choose the Master Word that shows a similar relation to the word(s) preceding the blank.

1. frugal	:spendthrift	::unrepentant	:	_____
2. ruffian	:brute	::banned	:	_____
3. ruffled	:pleased	::blending	:	_____
4. amiable	:unsociable	::refreshed	:	_____
5. wield	:employ	::soak	:	_____
6. prominent	:undistinguished	::happy	:	_____
7. imply	:indicate	::clothing	:	_____
8. superiority	:lowliness	::slight	:	_____
9. abstemious	:moderate	::stifling	:	_____
10. despotic	:dictatorial	::hopelessness	:	_____

EXERCISE 5

The Master Words in this lesson are repeated below. From the Master Words, choose the appropriate word for the blank in each of the following sentences. Write the word in the numbered space provided at the right.

| close | dire | garb | penitential | steep |
| despondency | dissonance | melancholy | spent | taboo |

1. After the long march, he was ...?... and dropped on the grass and went to sleep. 1._____

2. ...?... is often the state of mind in the late stages of mental illness. 2._____

3. Let the roast ...?... in its own sweet juices for at least an hour. 3._____

4. In the jungle, the air is so ...?... that one can scarcely breathe. 4._____

5. Rock music often contains ...?..., which grates on some listeners' nerves. 5._____

6. In some societies, a skirt is perfectly acceptable ...?... for men. 6._____

7. After a naughty deed, children may behave in (a, an) ...?... manner and ask forgiveness. 7._____

8. You can choose not to work in life, but to do so usually results in ...?... consequences. 8._____

9. Poe's poetry gets much of its ...?... tone from his subject matter, frequently the death of a beautiful woman. 9._____

10. Wearing jeans in our school on "dress-up day" is ...?... . 10._____

EXERCISE 6

To complete this puzzle, fill in the Master Word associated with each phrase below. Then unscramble the circled letters to form a Master Word from Lesson 10, and define it.

1. forbidden fruit, for instance — —Ⓞ— —
2. what you might be after a hard day — — — —
3. a crowded room may be this way — — — —Ⓞ
4. you might do this to tea — — — —
5. a uniform or costume —Ⓞ— —
6. a person with regrets feels this way — — — — — — — — —Ⓞ
7. what an orchestra out of tune produces — — — — —Ⓞ— —
8. like an extreme need, for example —Ⓞ— —
9. end-of-the-world attitude — — — — — — — — — —
10. feeling "blue" Ⓞ— — — — — — — —

Unscrambled word: _____

Definition: _____

LESSON 12   Review of Lessons 1–11

Part I: From the list below, choose the appropriate word for each sentence that follows. Use each word only once.

clamor	dissonance	garb	parch
debris	emaciated	huddled	privilege
despotic	etched	myriad	stamina

1. The swimmer possessed so much _____ that she continued to gain speed while the others were slowing down.

2. With the threat of tornadoes looming, we _____ together in our basement.

3. The desert wind and the midday sun will _____ even a hardy hiker.

4. The ruler's overwhelming power was considered _____ by some of his subjects.

5. The strain of the ordeal was _____ on his face.

6. Though the _____ of the grade school orchestra hurt their ears, the audience applauded heartily.

7. Meeting the president was a(n) _____ I never expected to have.

8. An overly strict diet may lead to (a, an) _____ condition.

9. Above all the _____ at the convention, one delegate shouted to be heard.

10. People spent hours cleaning up the _____ from the huge company picnic.

11. After the accident, several eyewitnesses offered police _____ points of view.

12. Tarzan's _____ is so familiar that he would look strange dressed in a business suit.

Part II: From the list below, choose the appropriate word for each sentence that follows. Use each word only once.

conflagration	dread	exclusion	recall
despondency	elite	frugal	spout
dislodge	evokes	magnitude	statistical

1. The financier Worthington was in a state of _____ when the stock market crashed.

2. A tall _____ of steam emerged from the geyser.

3. The wealthy couple was considered part of New York society's _____.

4. The _____ ignited other buildings, and an entire block was destroyed.

5. It was with utter _____ that I drove the smashed-up car into the driveway.

6. I only listened to my friend Manny's advice, to the _____ of everyone else's.

7. Consuelo remarked that she had a dim _____ of what happened before the accident.

8. Ben's scanty wardrobe hinted that he was _____ with his money.

9. The expert used _____ data to show a population increase.

10. The engineer attempted to _____ the huge rock with dynamite.

11. So great is the _____ of the pollution problem that the damage is almost irreparable.

12. The picture _____ pleasant memories of last summer's camping trip.

Part III: Decide whether the first pair in the items below are synonyms or antonyms. Then choose a Master Word from Lessons 1–11 that shows a similar relation to the word(s) preceding the blank. Do not repeat a Master Word that appears in the first column.

1. prone	:apt	::destroyed	: _____
2. prominent	:outstanding	::various	: _____
3. clamor	:peace	::slim	: _____
4. resolute	:determined	::gigantic	: _____
5. fidelity	:loyalty	::cowered	: _____
6. distracted	:inattentive	::courtesy	: _____
7. elite	:first-class	::clothing	: _____
8. wield	:manage	::self-restrained	: _____
9. amiable	:pleasant	::magician	: _____
10. lavishly	:generously	::decision	: _____
11. precise	:vague	::unhidden	: _____
12. pentitential	:shameless	::soothed	: _____
13. dread	:anticipation	::foolishness	: _____
14. cunning	:bumbling	::erected	: _____
15. lurid	:subdued	::merciful	: _____
16. emaciated	:nourished	::finite	: _____
17. bolster	:deflate	::unthrifty	: _____
18. occupied	:settled	::rubble	: _____
19. starkly	:grimly	::placed	: _____
20. reassure	:hearten	::halted	: _____

Read the following selection to get the general meaning. Read it a second time, paying special attention to the words in dark type. Notice how they are used in sentences. These are Master Words. These are the words you will be working with in this lesson.

From **The Last of the Mohicans**
by James Fenimore Cooper

It was a feature **peculiar** to the colonial wars of North America, that the toils and dangers of the wilderness were to be encountered before the adverse hosts could meet. A wide and apparently an **impervious** boundary of forests **severed** the possessions of the hostile provinces of France and England. The hardy colonist, and the trained European who fought at his side, frequently **expended** months in struggling against the rapids of the streams, or in **effecting** the rugged passes of the mountains, in quest of an opportunity to exhibit their courage in a more **martial** conflict. But, **emulating** the patience and self-denial of the practiced native warriors, they learned to overcome every difficulty; and it would seem that, in time, there was no **recess** of the woods so dark, nor any secret place so lonely, that it might claim **exemption** from the inroads of those who had pledged their blood to **satiate** their vengeance, or to uphold the cold and selfish policy of the distant monarchs of Europe.

Perhaps no district throughout the wide extent of the intermediate frontiers can furnish a livelier picture of the cruelty and fierceness of the savage warfare of those periods than the country which lies between the head waters of the Hudson and the adjacent lakes.

The facilities which nature had there offered to the march of the combatants were too obvious to be neglected. The lengthened sheet of the Champlain stretched from the frontiers of Canada, deep within the borders of the neighboring province of New York.

EXERCISE 1

SELF-TEST: After reading the above selection, do the following. Look at the Master Words below. Underline the words that you think you know. Circle the words that you are less sure about. Draw a square around the words you don't recognize.

MASTER WORDS

effect	**martial**
emulate	**peculiar**
exemption	**recess**
expend	**satiate**
impervious	**sever**

Read the selection on the preceding page again, this time paying special attention to the ten Master Words. In the (a) spaces provided below, write down what you think is the meaning of the word. After you have attempted a definition for each word, look up the word in a dictionary. In the (b) spaces, copy the appropriate dictionary definition.

1. **effect** (v.)

    a. _____

    b. _____

2. **emulate** (v.)

    a. _____

    b. _____

3. **exemption** (n.)

    a. _____

    b. _____

4. **expend** (v.)

    a. _____

    b. _____

5. **impervious** (adj.)

    a. _____

    b. _____

6. **martial** (adj.)

    a. _____

    b. _____

7. **peculiar** (adj.)

    a. _____

    b. _____

8. **recess** (n.)

    a. _____

    b. _____

9. **satiate** (v.)

    a. _____

    b. _____

10. **sever** (v.)

    a. _____

    b. _____

EXERCISE 3

Use the following list of synonyms and antonyms to fill in the blanks. Some words have no antonyms. In such cases, the antonym blanks have been marked with an X.

accomplish	imitate	originate	starve
cut	impenetrable	peaceful	tie
exclusion	inclusion	projection	unusual
fail	indentation	save	vulnerable
gorge	ordinary	spend	warlike

	Synonyms	Antonyms
1. **peculiar**		
2. **impervious**		
3. **sever**		
4. **expend**		
5. **effect**		
6. **martial**		
7. **emulate**		
8. **recess**		
9. **exemption**		
10. **satiate**		

EXERCISE 4

Decide whether the first pair in the items below are synonyms or antonyms. Then choose the Master Word that shows a similar relation to the word(s) preceding the blank.

1. garb :attire ::nook : _____
2. penitential :unremorseful ::create : _____
3. despondency :despair ::separate : _____
4. melancholy :joyous ::nonviolent : _____
5. spent :revived ::unguarded : _____
6. taboo :prohibited ::achieve : _____
7. steep :brew ::exception : _____
8. dire :minor ::common : _____
9. dissonance :harmony ::reserve : _____
10. close :muggy ::overfeed : _____

49   LESSON THIRTEEN

The Master Words in this lesson are repeated below. From the Master Words, choose the appropriate word for the blank in each of the following sentences. Write the word in the numbered space provided at the right.

effect	exemption	impervious	peculiar	satiate
emulate	expend	martial	recess	sever

1. The governor declared ...?... law to exist after the flood rolled through the lowland.

1. _____

2. ...?... those who do quality work to improve your own production.

2. _____

3. The treasure was hidden in the ...?... of the cave.

3. _____

4. Everyone is allowed at least one ...?... on the federal income tax form.

4. _____

5. Knights were rarely wounded because armor made them ...?... to blows.

5. _____

6. After the duke was assassinated, the country decided to ...?... its ties with the Balkan countries.

6. _____

7. Our country will have to ...?... an estimated $30 billion in order to improve the environment significantly.

7. _____

8. The company's personnel department promised to ...?... the hiring policy changes immediately.

8. _____

9. A six-inch rainfall will so ...?... the soil that we will need sand-bags to hold the runoff.

9. _____

10. Nonconforming people may seem ...?... to those who consider themselves well adjusted.

10. _____

Write the Master Word that is associated with each word group below. Then list three things that might be associated with the review word that follows.

1. waterproof, airtight, "nerves of steel"   _____

2. apron strings, divorce, guillotine   _____

3. role models, knock-off brand, mimic   _____

4. offbeat, bizarre, quirky   _____

5. time, energy, resources   _____

6. niche, cranny, hollow   _____

7. changes, results, by-products   _____

8. excess riches, indigestion, pig out   _____

9. religious, tax, medical   _____

10. arms, battalion, soldier   _____

Review word: garb (Lesson 11)

_____   _____   _____

Read the following selection to get the general meaning. Read it a second time, paying special attention to the words in dark type. Notice how they are used in sentences. These are Master Words. These are the words you will be working with in this lesson.

From **Spring in Mesopotamia**
by Austin Layard

Flowers of every **hue** enamelled the meadows; not thinly scattered over the grass as in northern climes, but in such thick and gathering clusters that the whole plain seemed a patchwork of many colors. The dogs, as they returned from hunting, **issued** from the long grass dyed red, yellow, or blue, according to the flowers through which they had last forced their way.

The villages of Naifa and Nimroud were deserted, and I remained alone with Said and my servants. The houses now began to swarm with vermin. We no longer slept under the roofs, and it was time to follow the example of the Arabs. I accordingly encamped on the edge of a large pond on the outskirts of Nimroud. Said accompanied me; and Salah, his young wife, a bright-eyed Arab girl, built up his shed, and watched and milked his **diminutive** flock of sheep and goats. . . .

As the sun went down behind the low hills which separate the river from the desert—even their rocky sides had struggled to emulate the **verdant** clothing of the plain—its **receding** rays were gradually withdrawn, like a **transparent** veil of light, from the landscape. . . . Sometimes a party of horsemen might have been seen in the distance slowly crossing the plain, the tufts of ostrich feathers which topped their long spears showing darkly against the evening sky. They would ride up to my tent, and give me the usual **salutation,** "Peace be with you, O Bey," or "Allah Aienak, God help you." Then driving the end of their lances into the ground, they would spring from their mares, and fasten their halters to the still quivering weapons. Seating themselves on the grass, they related deeds of war and **plunder,** or **speculated** on the site of the tents of Sofuk, until the moon rose, when they **vaulted** into their saddles, and took the way of the desert.

EXERCISE 1

SELF-TEST: After reading the above selection, do the following. Look at the Master Words below. Underline the words that you think you know. Circle the words that you are less sure about. Draw a square around the words you don't recognize.

MASTER WORDS

diminutive	salutation
hue	speculate
issue	transparent
plunder	vault
recede	verdant

Read the selection on the preceding page again, this time paying special attention to the ten Master Words. In the (a) spaces provided below, write down what you think is the meaning of the word. After you have attempted a definition for each word, look up the word in a dictionary. In the (b) spaces, copy the appropriate dictionary definition.

1. **diminutive** (adj.)

   a. _____

   b. _____

2. **hue** (n.)

   a. _____

   b. _____

3. **issue** (v.)

   a. _____

   b. _____

4. **plunder** (n.)

   a. _____

   b. _____

5. **recede** (v.)

   a. _____

   b. _____

6. **salutation** (n.)

   a. _____

   b. _____

7. **speculate** (v.)

   a. _____

   b. _____

8. **transparent** (adj.)

   a. _____

   b. _____

9. **vault** (v.)

   a. _____

   b. _____

10. **verdant** (adj.)

   a. _____

   b. _____

Use the following list of synonyms and antonyms to fill in the blanks. Some words have no antonyms. In such cases, the antonym blanks have been marked with an X.

advance	emerge	opaque	prove
barren	green	pallor	restoration
clear	greeting	pillage	retreat
climb	leap	ponder	snub
color	little	prodigious	withdraw

	Synonyms	**Antonyms**
1. **hue**	_____	_____
2. **transparent**	_____	_____
3. **issue**	_____	_____
4. **diminutive**	_____	_____
5. **recede**	_____	_____
6. **verdant**	_____	_____
7. **salutation**	_____	_____
8. **plunder**	_____	_____
9. **speculate**	_____	_____
10. **vault**	_____	_____

EXERCISE 4 ▰▰▰▰▰▰▰▰▰▰▰▰▰▰▰▰▰▰▰▰▰▰▰▰▰▰

Decide whether the first pair in the items below are synonyms or antonyms. Then choose the Master Word that shows a similar relation to the word(s) preceding the blank.

1. emulate	:invent	::clouded	: _____
2. effect	:produce	::tint	: _____
3. peculiar	:usual	::verify	: _____
4. exemption	:immunity	::appear	: _____
5. recess	:indentation	::destruction	: _____
6. impervious	:defenseless	::proceed	: _____
7. expend	:withhold	::colossal	: _____
8. sever	:divide	::jump	: _____
9. satiate	:overload	::grassy	: _____
10. martial	:peacemaking	::farewell	: _____

The Master Words in this lesson are repeated below. From the Master Words, choose the appropriate word for the blank in each of the following sentences. Write the word in the numbered space provided at the right.

| diminutive | issue | recede | speculate | vault |
| hue | plunder | salutation | transparent | verdant |

1. The golden ...?... of the baby's hair faded to a light brown color when he grew older.

1. _____

2. The poor conditions of the treasury caused him to ...?... on what things would be like in another year.

2. _____

3. The waters are most likely to ...?... before it rains again.

3. _____

4. Who was responsible for the ...?... of the villages north of Rome?

4. _____

5. The soldiers had to ...?... over the last barrier of the obstacle course and sprint the last fifty yards.

5. _____

6. A pitcher who is less than six feet tall is now considered ...?... by big league standards.

6. _____

7. The ...?... of the letter helps to set the tone.

7. _____

8. England's ...?... meadows are so rich and lush that one can walk ankle-deep in dew-laden grass for miles.

8. _____

9. The packaging is ...?... so customers can see the product.

9. _____

10. The teacher is expected to ...?... a bulletin explaining the details of the test program.

10. _____

Fill in the chart below with the Master Word that fits each set of clues. Part of speech refers to the word's usage in the lesson. Use a dictionary when necessary.

Number of Syllables	Part of Speech	Other Clues	Master Word
1	noun	a rainbow has more than one	1. _____
4	noun	a smile and a wave	2. _____
2	adjective	like a summer forest	3. _____
2	verb	sprout or stem from, for example	4. _____
1	verb	cheerleaders do this	5. _____
3	verb	make an educated guess	6. _____
3	adjective	like glass	7. _____
2	verb	hairlines may do this	8. _____
4	adjective	pint-sized	9. _____
2	noun	a raid, for example	10. _____

Read the following selection to get the general meaning. Read it a second time, paying special attention to the words in dark type. Notice how they are used in sentences. These are Master Words. These are the words you will be working with in this lesson.

From **"A Washoe Joke"**
by Mark Twain

A petrified man was found some time ago in the mountains south of Gravelly Ford. Every limb and feature of the stony mummy was perfect, not even excepting the left leg, which has evidently been a wooden one during the lifetime of the owner—which lifetime, by the way, came to a close about a century ago, in the opinion of *savan* [a wise person] who has examined the **defunct.** The body was in a sitting posture and leaning against a huge mass of croppings; the attitude was **pensive,** the right thumb resting against the side of the nose; the left thumb partially supported the chin, the forefinger pressing the inner corner of the left eye and drawing it partly open; the right eye was closed, and the fingers of the right hand spread apart. This strange freak of nature created a **profound** sensation in the vicinity, and our informant states that, by request, Justice Sewell or Sowell of Humboldt City at once proceeded to the spot and held an **inquest** on the body. The **verdict** of the jury was that "deceased came to his death from **protracted** exposure," etc. The people of the neighborhood volunteered to bury the poor unfortunate, and were even anxious to do so; but it was discovered, when they attempted to remove him, that the water which had dripped upon him for ages from the **crag** above, had coursed down his back and deposited a limestone **sediment** under him which had glued him to the bedrock upon which he sat, as with a cement of **adamant,** and Judge S. refused to allow the charitable citizens to blast him from his position. The opinion expressed by his Honor that such a course would be little less than **sacrilege,** was eminently just and proper. Everybody goes to see the stone man, as many as 300 persons having visited the hardened creature during the past five or six weeks.

EXERCISE 1

SELF-TEST: After reading the above selection, do the following. Look at the Master Words below. Underline the words that you think you know. Circle the words that you are less sure about. Draw a square around the words you don't recognize.

MASTER WORDS

adamant	**profound**
crag	**protract**
defunct	**sacrilege**
inquest	**sediment**
pensive	**verdict**

Read the selection on the preceding page again, this time paying special attention to the ten Master Words. In the (a) spaces provided below, write down what you think is the meaning of the word. After you have attempted a definition for each word, look up the word in a dictionary. In the (b) spaces, copy the appropriate dictionary definition.

1. **adamant** (n.)

    a. _____

    b. _____

2. **crag** (n.)

    a. _____

    b. _____

3. **defunct** (adj.)

    a. _____

    b. _____

4. **inquest** (n.)

    a. _____

    b. _____

5. **pensive** (adj.)

    a. _____

    b. _____

6. **profound** (adj.)

    a. _____

    b. _____

7. **protract** (v.)

    a. _____

    b. _____

8. **sacrilege** (n.)

    a. _____

    b. _____

9. **sediment** (n.)

    a. _____

    b. _____

10. **verdict** (n.)

    a. _____

    b. _____

Use the following list of synonyms and antonyms to fill in the blanks. Some words have no antonyms. In such cases, the antonym blanks have been marked with an X.

blasphemy	curtail	inoperative	ravine
clay	deadlock	investigation	reverence
cliff	deep	judgment	shallow
contemplative	dregs	operational	unthinking
cover-up	granite	prolong	

	Synonyms	**Antonyms**
1. **defunct**	_____	_____
2. **pensive**	_____	_____
3. **profound**	_____	_____
4. **inquest**	_____	_____
5. **verdict**	_____	_____
6. **protract**	_____	_____
7. **crag**	_____	_____
8. **sediment**	_____	X
9. **adamant**	_____	_____
10. **sacrilege**	_____	_____

Decide whether the first pair in the items below are synonyms or antonyms. Then choose the Master Word that shows a similar relation to the word(s) preceding the blank.

1. salutation	:send-off	::shorten	: _____
2. plunder	:ransacking	::inquiry	: _____
3. hue	:shade	::stone	: _____
4. transparent	:cloudy	::functional	: _____
5. diminutive	:huge	::thoughtless	: _____
6. verdant	:grass-green	::settlings	: _____
7. recede	:approach	::meaningless	: _____
8. vault	:hurdle	::decision	: _____
9. issue	:arise	::bluff	: _____
10. speculate	:demonstrate	::worship	: _____

LESSON FIFTEEN

The Master Words in this lesson are repeated below. From the Master Words, choose the appropriate word for the blank in each of the following sentences. Write the word in the numbered space provided at the right.

adamant	defunct	pensive	protract	sediment
crag	inquest	profound	sacrilege	verdict

1. Rich ...?... thickly coated the riverbed.   1. _____

2. He was rock-ribbed—made of ...?...—and never yielded in battle.   2. _____

3. Greg's trivial objections always ...?... our club meetings.   3. _____

4. The coroner gathered information during the ...?... .   4. _____

5. Some people think putting a book upside down on a shelf is (a, an) ...?... .   5. _____

6. The most ...?... thinkers are often reluctant to make hasty judgments.   6. _____

7. Poets need (a, an) ...?... mood for reaching a proper emotional pitch to write.   7. _____

8. The plane crash that claimed 30 lives occurred on a mountain ...?... deep in the Rockies.   8. _____

9. The company that once produced boxcars is now ...?..., and the directors have filed for bankruptcy.   9. _____

10. The foreman said the jury would have (a, an) ...?... in two hours.   10. _____

To complete the crossword, choose the Master Word associated with each word or phrase below. Begin each answer in the square having the same number as the clue.

1. like a wistful child, for example

2. grounds in the bottom of a coffee cup

3. to draw out an argument, for example

4. theft from a church

5. long gone

6. unbreakable rock

7. Einstein's theories were this

8. might challenge a mountain climber

9. what a grand jury might conduct

10. the final word

Read the following selection to get the general meaning. Read it a second time, paying special attention to the words in dark type. Notice how they are used in sentences. These are Master Words. These are the words you will be working with in this lesson.

From **The Scarlet Letter**
by Nathaniel Hawthorne

After her return to the prison, Hester Prynne was found to be in a state of nervous excitement that demanded constant watchfulness lest she should **perpetrate** violence on herself, or do some half-frenzied mischief to the poor babe. As night approached, it proving impossible to **quell** her **insubordination** by **rebuke** or threats of punishment, Master Brackett, the jailer, thought fit to introduce a physician. He described him as a man of skill in all Christian modes of physical science, and likewise familiar with whatever the savage people could teach, in respect to medicinal herbs and roots that grew in the forest. To say the truth, there was much need of professional assistance, not merely for Hester herself, but still more **urgently** for the child; who, drawing its sustenance from the maternal bosom, seemed to have drunk in with it all the **turmoil,** the **anguish** and despair, which **pervaded** the mother's system. It now **writhed** in convulsions of pain, and was a forcible type in its little frame, of the moral agony which Hester Prynne had **borne** throughout the day.

Closely following the jailer into the dismal apartment appeared that individual of singular aspect, whose presence in the crowd had been of such deep interest to the wearer of the scarlet letter. He was lodged in the prison, not as suspected of any offence, but as the most convenient and suitable mode of disposing of him until the magistrates should have conferred with the Indian sagamores respecting his ransom. His name was announced as Roger Chillingworth.

EXERCISE 1

SELF-TEST: After reading the above selection, do the following. Look at the Master Words below. Underline the words that you think you know. Circle the words that you are less sure about. Draw a square around the words you don't recognize.

MASTER WORDS

anguish	quell
bear	rebuke
insubordination	turmoil
perpetrate	urgent
pervade	writhe

Read the selection on the preceding page again, this time paying special attention to the ten Master Words. In the (a) spaces provided below, write down what you think is the meaning of the word. After you have attempted a definition for each word, look up the word in a dictionary. In the (b) spaces, copy the appropriate dictionary definition.

1. **anguish** (n.)

   a. _____

   b. _____

2. **bear** (v.)

   a. _____

   b. _____

3. **insubordination** (n.)

   a. _____

   b. _____

4. **perpetrate** (v.)

   a. _____

   b. _____

5. **pervade** (v.)

   a. _____

   b. _____

6. **quell** (v.)

   a. _____

   b. _____

7. **rebuke** (n.)

   a. _____

   b. _____

8. **turmoil** (n.)

   a. _____

   b. _____

9. **urgent** (adj.)

   a. _____

   b. _____

10. **writhe** (v.)

   a. _____

   b. _____

Use the following list of synonyms and antonyms to fill in the blanks. Some words have no antonyms. In such cases, the antonym blanks have been marked with an X.

agitation	contemplate	misery	support
approval	defiance	obedience	tranquillity
collapse	important	rapture	twist
commit	incite	reprimand	uncoil
condense	infiltrate	subdue	unnecessary

	Synonyms	**Antonyms**
1. **perpetrate**	_____	_____
2. **quell**	_____	_____
3. **insubordination**	_____	_____
4. **rebuke**	_____	_____
5. **urgent**	_____	_____
6. **turmoil**	_____	_____
7. **anguish**	_____	_____
8. **pervade**	_____	_____
9. **writhe**	_____	_____
10. **bear**	_____	_____

Decide whether the first pair in the items below are synonyms or antonyms. Then choose the Master Word that shows a similar relation to the word(s) preceding the blank.

1. sacrilege	:blessing	::needless	: _____
2. profound	:trivial	::stir up	: _____
3. pensive	:distracted	::loyalty	: _____
4. adamant	:rock	::carry	: _____
5. defunct	:active	::pleasure	: _____
6. protract	:reduce	::peace	: _____
7. sediment	:residue	::scolding	: _____
8. verdict	:conclusion	::squirm	: _____
9. inquest	:probe	::spread	: _____
10. crag	:cliff	::perform	: _____

The Master Words in this lesson are repeated below. From the Master Words, choose the appropriate word for the blank in each of the following sentences. Write the word in the numbered space provided at the right.

anguish	insubordination	pervade	rebuke	urgent
bear	perpetrate	quell	turmoil	writhe

1. The National Guard was able to ...?... the riot in about two hours.   1. _____

2. "In two minutes," the villain warned, "the poisonous gas will completely ...?... the room."   2. _____

3. The lieutenant charged the insolent private with ...?... .   3. _____

4. For not wearing his helmet in the car, the officer received a mild ...?... from the commissioner.   4. _____

5. Each person in life has a cross to ...?... .   5. _____

6. After he eats the deadly nightshade, he will ...?... in pain until the antidote is administered.   6. _____

7. Police said the felon would ...?... any crime without remorse.   7. _____

8. Envelopes marked "...?..." probably move no faster in the mail than any other envelope.   8. _____

9. The fighting on the field caused ...?... in the stands as well.   9. _____

10. The ...?... on the face of the young mother told the story of the little boy's death.   10. _____

Use at least five Master Words from this lesson to write a scene about one of the following topics. Or create a topic of your own. Write your choice on the blank. Circle the Master Words as you use them.

Possible Topics: Practical Joke, Rebellion in the Ranks

_____

_____

_____

_____

_____

_____

_____

_____

Read the following selection to get the general meaning. Read it a second time, paying special attention to the words in dark type. Notice how they are used in sentences. These are Master Words. These are the words you will be working with in this lesson.

From "A Branch-Road"
by Hamlin Garland

Potatoes were **seized,** cut in halves, **sopped** in gravy, and taken *one, two!* Corn cakes went into great jaws like coal into a steam-engine. Knives in the right hand cut and scooped gravy up. Great, muscular, grimy, but wholesome fellows they were, feeding like ancient Norse, and capable of working like demons. They were deep in the process, half-hidden by steam from the potatoes and stew, in less than sixty seconds from their entrance.

With a **shrinking** from the comments of the others upon his regard for Agnes, Will **assumed** a **reserved** and almost **haughty** air toward his fellow-workmen, and a curious coldness toward her. As he went in, she came forward smiling brightly.

"There's one more place, Will." A tender, **involuntary** droop in her voice betrayed her, and Will felt a wave of hot blood **surge** over him as the rest roared.

"Ha, ha! Oh, there'd be a place for *him!*"

"Don't worry, Will! Always room for *you* here!"

Will took his seat with a sudden, angry flame.

"Why can't she keep it from these fools?" was his thought. He didn't even thank her for showing him the chair.

She flushed **vividly,** but smiled back. She was so proud and happy, she didn't care very much if they *did* know it. But as Will looked at her with that quick, angry glance, and took his seat with scowling brow, she was hurt and puzzled. She redoubled her **exertions** to please him, and by so doing added to the amusement of the crowd that gnawed chicken-bones, rattled cups, knives and forks, and joked as they ate with small grace and no material loss of time.

EXERCISE 1

SELF-TEST: After reading the above selection, do the following. Look at the Master Words below. Underline the words that you think you know. Circle the words that you are less sure about. Draw a square around the words you don't recognize.

MASTER WORDS

assume	**seize**
exertion	**shrink**
haughty	**sop**
involuntary	**surge**
reserved	**vivid**

Read the selection on the preceding page again, this time paying special attention to the ten Master Words. In the (a) spaces provided below, write down what you think is the meaning of the word. After you have attempted a definition for each word, look up the word in a dictionary. In the (b) spaces, copy the appropriate dictionary definition.

1. **assume** (v.)

    a. _____

    b. _____

2. **exertion** (n.)

    a. _____

    b. _____

3. **haughty** (adj.)

    a. _____

    b. _____

4. **involuntary** (adj.)

    a. _____

    b. _____

5. **reserved** (adj.)

    a. _____

    b. _____

6. **seize** (v.)

    a. _____

    b. _____

7. **shrink** (v.)

    a. _____

    b. _____

8. **sop** (v.)

    a. _____

    b. _____

9. **surge** (v.)

    a. _____

    b. _____

10. **vivid** (adj.)

    a. _____

    b. _____

Use the following list of synonyms and antonyms to fill in the blanks. Some words have no antonyms. In such cases, the antonym blanks have been marked with an X.

affect	diffident	humble	stretch
arrogant	dull	idleness	trickle
automatic	flamboyant	intentional	unmask
bold	grab	liberate	work
contract	gush	soak	wring

	Synonyms	**Antonyms**
1. **seize**	_____	_____
2. **sop**	_____	_____
3. **shrink**	_____	_____
4. **assume**	_____	_____
5. **reserved**	_____	_____
6. **haughty**	_____	_____
7. **involuntary**	_____	_____
8. **surge**	_____	_____
9. **vivid**	_____	_____
10. **exertion**	_____	_____

Decide whether the first pair in the items below are synonyms or antonyms. Then choose the Master Word that shows a similar relation to the word(s) preceding the blank.

1. quell	:inflame	::willful	: _____
2. perpetrate	:commit	::nab	: _____
3. anguish	:enjoyment	::inactivity	: _____
4. urgent	:unimportant	::faded	: _____
5. insubordination	:respect	::modest	: _____
6. bear	:shoulder	::pretend	: _____
7. pervade	:penetrate	::recoil	: _____
8. writhe	:wriggle	::rush	: _____
9. turmoil	:calm	::outspoken	: _____
10. rebuke	:blame	::absorb	: _____

The Master Words in this lesson are repeated below. From the Master Words, choose the appropriate word for the blank in each of the following sentences. Write the word in the numbered space provided at the right.

assume	haughty	reserved	shrink	surge
exertion	involuntary	seize	sop	vivid

1. Police ...?...(d, ed) the mobsters in an old garage near the town.   1. _____

2. If we ...?... his bread in milk, Shep is contented when he eats.   2. _____

3. Thomas Paine noted that "summer soldiers" ...?... from service to country in time of national stress.   3. _____

4. Blinking of the eyes is usually (a, an) ...?... act, like sneezing or breathing.   4. _____

5. As a beginning, the artist sprayed the canvas with ...?... colors.   5. _____

6. Shoveling snow is often dangerous ...?... for the elderly.   6. _____

7. ...?... people, because they are not outgoing, present an image of dignity.   7. _____

8. ...?... generals—like General Patton—use a swagger stick as a prop.   8. _____

9. Unplug the computer in case the power should ...?... suddenly.   9. _____

10. To get the information, he had to ...?... the role of a runaway boy.   10. _____

The invented words below are formed from parts of different Master Words from this lesson. Create a definition and indicate the part of speech for each word. The first one is done for you.

reservedshrink   *(v.) to withdraw quietly and unemotionally* _____

exertshrink   _____

involunsume   _____

seizehaughty   _____

Now invent your own words by combining parts of the Master Words. Create a definition for each, and indicate the word's part of speech. (You may reuse any of the word parts above in new combinations.)

1. _____   _____

2. _____   _____

Read the following selection to get the general meaning. Read it a second time, paying special attention to the words in dark type. Notice how they are used in sentences. These are Master Words. These are the words you will be working with in this lesson.

From **"Recollections and Opinions of an Old Pioneer"** by Peter H. Burnett

A trip to Oregon with ox teams was at that time a new experiment, and was **exceedingly severe** upon the temper and endurance of people. It was one of the most **conclusive** tests of character, and the very best school in which to study human nature. Before the trip terminated, people acted upon their genuine **principles,** and threw off all disguises. It was not that the trip was beset with very great **perils,** for we had no war with the Indians, and no stock stolen by them. But there were ten thousand little **vexations** continually **recurring,** which could not be foreseen before they occurred, not fully remembered when past, but were keenly felt while passing. At one time an ox would be missing, at another time a mule, and then a struggle for the best encampment, and for a supply of wood and water; and, in these struggles, the worst **traits** of human nature were displayed, and there was no **remedy** but patient endurance. At the beginning of the journey there were several fisticuff fights in camp; but the emigrants soon abandoned that practice, and thereafter confined themselves to **abuse** in words only. The man with a black eye and battered face could not well hunt up his cattle or drive his team.

EXERCISE 1

SELF-TEST: After reading the above selection, do the following. Look at the Master Words below. Underline the words that you think you know. Circle the words that you are less sure about. Draw a square around the words you don't recognize.

MASTER WORDS

abuse	recur
conclusive	remedy
exceedingly	severe
peril	trait
principle	vexation

Read the selection on the preceding page again, this time paying special attention to the ten Master Words. In the (a) spaces provided below, write down what you think is the meaning of the word. After you have attempted a definition for each word, look up the word in a dictionary. In the (b) spaces, copy the appropriate dictionary definition.

1. **abuse** (v.)

    a. _____

    b. _____

2. **conclusive** (adj.)

    a. _____

    b. _____

3. **exceedingly** (adv.)

    a. _____

    b. _____

4. **peril** (n.)

    a. _____

    b. _____

5. **principle** (n.)

    a. _____

    b. _____

6. **recur** (v.)

    a. _____

    b. _____

7. **remedy** (n.)

    a. _____

    b. _____

8. **severe** (adj.)

    a. _____

    b. _____

9. **trait** (n.)

    a. _____

    b. _____

10. **vexation** (n.)

    a. _____

    b. _____

Use the following list of synonyms and antonyms to fill in the blanks. Some words have no antonyms. In such cases, the antonym blanks have been marked with an X.

abnormality	harassment	mistreat	rule
characteristic	harsh	panacea	safety
end	hazard	poison	satisfaction
excessively	insufficiently	praise	tentative
final	mild	return	

	Synonyms	**Antonyms**
1. **exceedingly**	_____	_____
2. **severe**	_____	_____
3. **conclusive**	_____	_____
4. **principle**	_____	X
5. **peril**	_____	_____
6. **vexation**	_____	_____
7. **recur**	_____	_____
8. **trait**	_____	_____
9. **abuse**	_____	_____
10. **remedy**	_____	_____

Decide whether the first pair in the items below are synonyms or antonyms. Then choose the Master Word that shows a similar relation to the word(s) preceding the blank.

1. sop	:mop up	::quality	: _____
2. shrink	:withdraw	::treatment	: _____
3. seize	:grasp	::repeat	: _____
4. vivid	:washed out	::gentle	: _____
5. surge	:swell	::irritation	: _____
6. exertion	:laziness	::respect	: _____
7. reserved	:outspoken	::security	: _____
8. haughty	:meek	::unproven	: _____
9. assume	:imitate	::belief	: _____
10. involuntary	:planned	::scarcely	: _____

LESSON EIGHTEEN

The Master Words in this lesson are repeated below. From the Master Words, choose the appropriate word for the blank in each of the following sentences. Write the word in the numbered space provided at the right.

| abuse | exceedingly | principle | remedy | trait |
| conclusive | peril | recur | severe | vexation |

1. The comedian's audience enjoyed his ...?... witty remarks and dry humor.   1._____

2. As a matter of ...?..., Anna never borrowed money from friends.   2._____

3. Drugs may get rid of the disease for a time, but you have no assurance the disease may not ...?... .   3._____

4. I saw ...?... on his face when he could not work the problem.   4._____

5. Teachers should not ...?... students with sarcasm.   5._____

6. Waiting in line for over an hour was (a, an) ...?... test of my patience.   6._____

7. Scientific people do not form strong opinions until the results of studies are ...?... .   7._____

8. All in all, a good attitude toward work is probably a more important ...?... than large amounts of talent.   8._____

9. Dancing lessons are sometimes (a, an) ...?... for those not naturally nimble on their feet.   9._____

10. Driving on tires with thin tread is a great ...?... on the highway.   10._____

EXERCISE 6 ▮▬▬▬▬▬▬▬▬▬▬▬▬▬▬▬▬▬▬▬▬▬▬▬

To complete the word spiral, choose the Master Word associated with each phrase below. Start with 1 and fill in each answer clockwise. Be careful! Each new word may overlap the previous word by one or more letters.

1. without a doubt

2. a pesky sibling might cause you this

3. a battle or a plague, for example

4. a dream or illness might do this

5. base your actions on this

6. to a great degree

7. height or hair color is an example

8. to injure with words

9. what winters are in the Arctic

10. cure-all

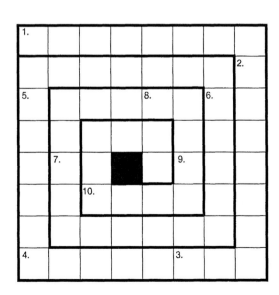

Read the following selection to get the general meaning. Read it a second time, paying special attention to the words in dark type. Notice how they are used in sentences. These are Master Words. These are the words you will be working with in this lesson.

From **Letters from an American Farmer**
by Hector St. John de Crévecoeur

In this great American **asylum,** the poor of Europe have by some means met together, and in **consequence** of various causes; to what purpose should they ask one another what countrymen they are? Alas, two thirds of them had no country. Can a **wretch** who wanders about, who works and starves, whose life is a **continual** scene of **sore affliction** or pinching **penury;** can that man call England or any other kingdom his country? A country that had no bread for him, whose fields procured him no harvest, who met with nothing but the frowns of the rich, the severity of the laws, with jails and punishments; who owned not a single foot of the **extensive** surface of this planet? No! urged by a variety of motives, here they came. Every thing has tended to **regenerate** them; new laws, a new mode of living, a new social system; here they are become men; in Europe they were as so many useless plants. . . . Formerly they were not numbered in any civil lists of their country except in those of the poor; here they rank as citizens. By what invisible power has this surprising **metamorphosis** been performed? By that of the laws and that of their industry.

EXERCISE 1

SELF-TEST: After reading the above selection, do the following. Look at the Master Words below. Underline the words that you think you know. Circle the words that you are less sure about. Draw a square around the words you don't recognize.

MASTER WORDS

affliction	metamorphosis
asylum	penury
consequence	regenerate
continual	sore
extensive	wretch

Read the selection on the preceding page again, this time paying special attention to the ten Master Words. In the (a) spaces provided below, write down what you think is the meaning of the word. After you have attempted a definition for each word, look up the word in a dictionary. In the (b) spaces, copy the appropriate dictionary definition.

1. **affliction** (n.)

    a. _____

    b. _____

2. **asylum** (n.)

    a. _____

    b. _____

3. **consequence** (n.)

    a. _____

    b. _____

4. **continual** (adj.)

    a. _____

    b. _____

5. **extensive** (adj.)

    a. _____

    b. _____

6. **metamorphosis** (n.)

    a. _____

    b. _____

7. **penury** (n.)

    a. _____

    b. _____

8. **regenerate** (v.)

    a. _____

    b. _____

9. **sore** (adj.)

    a. _____

    b. _____

10. **wretch** (n.)

    a. _____

    b. _____

Use the following list of synonyms and antonyms to fill in the blanks. Some words have no antonyms. In such cases, the antonym blanks have been marked with an X.

cause	intermittent	prison	transformation
changelessness	limited	renew	unfortunate
decay	opulence	result	uninterrupted
disease	painless	sanctuary	vast
health	poverty	tender	winner

	Synonyms	**Antonyms**
1. **asylum**	_____	_____
2. **consequence**	_____	_____
3. **wretch**	_____	_____
4. **continual**	_____	_____
5. **sore**	_____	_____
6. **affliction**	_____	_____
7. **penury**	_____	_____
8. **extensive**	_____	_____
9. **regenerate**	_____	_____
10. **metamorphosis**	_____	_____

EXERCISE 4 ▬▬▬▬▬▬▬▬▬▬▬▬▬

Decide whether the first pair in the items below are synonyms or antonyms. Then choose the Master Word that shows a similar relation to the word(s) preceding the blank.

1. conclusive	:undecided	::motive	:	_____
2. principle	:standard	::shelter	:	_____
3. abuse	:pamper	::fitness	:	_____
4. exceedingly	:hardly	::irregular	:	_____
5. recur	:reappear	::change	:	_____
6. peril	:protection	::narrow	:	_____
7. remedy	:cure	::reshape	:	_____
8. severe	:moderate	::wealth	:	_____
9. vexation	:frustration	::sufferer	:	_____
10. trait	:feature	::painful	:	_____

EXERCISE 5

The Master Words in this lesson are repeated below. From the Master Words, choose the appropriate word for the blank in each of the following sentences. Write the word in the numbered space provided at the right.

| affliction | consequence | extensive | penury | sore |
| asylum | continual | metamorphosis | regenerate | wretch |

1. Some Soviet defectors have sought ...?... in the United States and Sweden.

1. _____

2. In biology, we watch closely the ...?... of many examples from the plant kingdom.

2. _____

3. His study of Sanskrit had been as ...?... as any living scholar in the Western world.

3. _____

4. Some simple forms of life can ...?... to original size even though they may be cut completely in two.

4. _____

5. People who live in ...?... must think of staying alive before they think of getting an education.

5. _____

6. The marathon left very fit runners stiff and ...?... for days.

6. _____

7. Thoreau said that it is morally right to protest unjust laws, but we must be willing to suffer the ...?...(s).

7. _____

8. The poor ...?... lost both arms in the battle and was forced to beg for the rest of his life.

8. _____

9. The ...?... affecting the cattle seems to be a virus.

9. _____

10. His ...?... joking caused constant laughter in English class.

10. _____

EXERCISE 6

Write the Master Word that is associated with each word group below. Then list three things that might be associated with the review word that follows.

1. harbor, church, orphanage

_____

2. Cinderella, butterfly, Scrooge

_____

3. beggar, outcast, ragamuffin

_____

4. fallout, domino effect, aftermath

_____

5. skinned knee, bruised ego, painful memory

_____

6. homeless, bankrupt, penniless

_____

7. Fountain of Youth, exercise, spring

_____

8. Pacific Ocean, outer space, Sahara Desert

_____

9. plague, famine, insanity

_____

10. heartbeat, motor-mouth, leaky faucet

_____

Review word: severe (Lesson 18)

_____   _____   _____

LESSON 20

Read the following selection to get the general meaning. Read it a second time, paying special attention to the words in dark type. Notice how they are used in sentences. These are Master Words. These are the words you will be working with in this lesson.

From "Social Welfare and the Industrial Revolution" by Samuel Smiles

Sanitary objections were also urged in opposition to railways, and many wise doctors strongly **inveighed** against tunnels. Sir Anthony Carlisle insisted that "tunnels would expose healthy people to colds, catarrhs, and **consumption.**" The noise, the darkness, and the dangers of tunnel travelling were depicted in all their horrors. Worst of all, however, was "the destruction of the atmospheric air," as Dr. Lardner termed it. Elaborate **calculations** were made by that gentleman to prove that the provision of ventilating shafts would be altogether insufficient to prevent the dangers arising from the **combustion** of coke, producing carbonic acid gas, which, in large quantities, was fatal to life. He showed, for instance, that in the proposed Box Tunnel, on the Great Western Railway, the passage of a load of 100 tons would deposit about 3090 lbs. of **noxious** gases, incapable of supporting life! Here was an uncomfortable prospect of suffocation for passengers between London and Bristol. But steps were adopted to **allay** these **formidable** sources of terror. Solemn documents, in the form of certificates, were got up and published, signed by several of the most distinguished physicians of the day, **attesting** the perfect wholesomeness of tunnels, and the purity of the air in them. Perhaps they went further than was necessary in alleging, what certainly **subsequent** experience has not **verified,** that the atmosphere of the tunnel was "dry, of an agreeable temperature, and free from smell."

EXERCISE 1

SELF-TEST: After reading the above selection, do the following. Look at the Master Words below. Underline the words that you think you know. Circle the words that you are less sure about. Draw a square around the words you don't recognize.

MASTER WORDS

allay	formidable
attest	inveigh
calculation	noxious
combustion	subsequent
consumption	verify

Read the selection on the preceding page again, this time paying special attention to the ten Master Words. In the (a) spaces provided below, write down what you think is the meaning of the word. After you have attempted a definition for each word, look up the word in a dictionary. In the (b) spaces, copy the appropriate dictionary definition.

1. **allay** (v.)

    a. _____

    b. _____

2. **attest** (v.)

    a. _____

    b. _____

3. **calculation** (n.)

    a. _____

    b. _____

4. **combustion** (n.)

    a. _____

    b. _____

5. **consumption** (n.)

    a. _____

    b. _____

6. **formidable** (adj.)

    a. _____

    b. _____

7. **inveigh** (v.)

    a. _____

    b. _____

8. **noxious** (adj.)

    a. _____

    b. _____

9. **subsequent** (adj.)

    a. _____

    b. _____

10. **verify** (v.)

    a. _____

    b. _____

Use the following list of synonyms and antonyms to fill in the blanks. Some words have no antonyms. In such cases, the antonym blanks have been marked with an X.

aggravate	ease	innocuous	substantiate
attack	explosion	inviting	succeeding
computation	fearsome	preceding	testify
defend	guess	repudiate	tuberculosis
disavow	harmful	smothering	

	Synonyms	**Antonyms**
1. **inveigh**	_____	_____
2. **calculation**	_____	_____
3. **allay**	_____	_____
4. **combustion**	_____	_____
5. **noxious**	_____	_____
6. **consumption**	_____	X _____
7. **attest**	_____	_____
8. **formidable**	_____	_____
9. **subsequent**	_____	_____
10. **verify**	_____	_____

Decide whether the first pair in the items below are synonyms or antonyms. Then choose the Master Word that shows a similar relation to the word(s) preceding the blank.

1. asylum	:safety	::figuring	: _____
2. continual	:interrupted	::worsen	: _____
3. consequence	:stimulus	::contest	: _____
4. affliction	:well-being	::appealing	: _____
5. regenerate	:rebuild	::tuberculosis	: _____
6. wretch	:victim	::prove	: _____
7. penury	:riches	::harmless	: _____
8. extensive	:restricted	::support	: _____
9. sore	:aching	::following	: _____
10. metamorphosis	:evolution	::ignition	: _____

The Master Words in this lesson are repeated below. From the Master Words, choose the appropriate word for the blank in each of the following sentences. Write the word in the numbered space provided at the right.

allay	calculation	consumption	inveigh	subsequent
attest	combustion	formidable	noxious	verify

1. A quick ...?... will tell the cash value of your insurance policy.

1. _____

2. The first reports were discouraging, but ...?... accounts indicated we were doing better.

2. _____

3. Proper fuel ...?... plays a big role in the efficient operation of an engine.

3. _____

4. Hemp has been declared (a, an) ...?... plant in most states, and farmers are trying to wipe it out.

4. _____

5. Neither side could ...?... the number of casualties they claimed.

5. _____

6. John's mathematics ability should ...?... any fears you have that he shouldn't study engineering.

6. _____

7. When all seems wrong in a country, it is popular to ...?... against the government.

7. _____

8. Early detection has helped to cut deaths from ...?... .

8. _____

9. You will find Roger (a, an) ...?... opponent who will try to over-power anyone he plays against.

9. _____

10. I can ...?... to Tom's skill at golf after playing with him.

10. _____

To complete this puzzle, fill in the Master Word associated with each phrase below. Then unscramble the circled letters to form a Master Word from Lesson 19, and define it.

1. gas fumes and poison ivy

     — — — — — Ⓞ —

2. a lung disease

     — Ⓞ — — — — — — —

3. a spark may cause this

     — Ⓞ — — — — — — —

4. to state under oath, for instance

     — — Ⓞ — — —

5. coming after

     — — — — — — — — — —

6. show positive proof

     — — — Ⓞ — — —

7. a mathematical effort

     Ⓞ — — — — — — — — — —

8. like Mt. Everest or a marathon

     — — — — — — — — Ⓞ —

9. to tongue-lash

     — Ⓞ — — — — —

10. to ease pain or fear, for example

     Ⓞ — — — —

Unscrambled word: _____

Definition: _____

Read the following selection to get the general meaning. Read it a second time, paying special attention to the words in dark type. Notice how they are used in sentences. These are Master Words. These are the words you will be working with in this lesson.

From **"The Blue Hotel"**
by Stephen Crane

At last, Scully, **elaborately,** with **boisterous** hospitality, conducted them through the **portals** of the blue hotel. The room which they entered was small. It seemed to be merely a proper temple for an enormous stove, which, in the center, was humming with godlike violence. At various points on its surface the iron had become **luminous** and glowed yellow from the heat. Beside the stove Scully's son Johnnie was playing High-Five with an old farmer who had whiskers both gray and sandy. They were quarrelling. Frequently the old farmer turned his face toward a box of sawdust—colored brown from tobacco juice—that was behind the stove, and spat with an air of great impatience and irritation. With a loud **flourish** of words Scully destroyed the game of cards, and bustled his son upstairs with part of the baggage of the new guests. He himself conducted them to three basins of the coldest water in the world. The cowboy and the Easterner **burnished** themselves fiery red with this water, until it seemed to be some kind of metal polish. The Swede, however, merely dipped his fingers **gingerly** and with **trepidation.** It was notable that throughout this series of small ceremonies the three travellers were made to feel that Scully was very **benevolent.** He was conferring great favors upon them. He handed the towel from one to another with an air of **philanthropic** impulse.

EXERCISE 1

SELF-TEST: After reading the above selection, do the following. Look at the Master Words below. Underline the words that you think you know. Circle the words that you are less sure about. Draw a square around the words you don't recognize.

MASTER WORDS

benevolent	**gingerly**
boisterous	**luminous**
burnish	**philanthropic**
elaborately	**portal**
flourish	**trepidation**

Read the selection on the preceding page again, this time paying special attention to the ten Master Words. In the (a) spaces provided below, write down what you think is the meaning of the word. After you have attempted a definition for each word, look up the word in a dictionary. In the (b) spaces, copy the appropriate dictionary definition.

1. **benevolent** (adj.)

   a. _____

   b. _____

2. **boisterous** (adj.)

   a. _____

   b. _____

3. **burnish** (v.)

   a. _____

   b. _____

4. **elaborately** (adv.)

   a. _____

   b. _____

5. **flourish** (n.)

   a. _____

   b. _____

6. **gingerly** (adv.)

   a. _____

   b. _____

7. **luminous** (adj.)

   a. _____

   b. _____

8. **philanthropic** (adj.)

   a. _____

   b. _____

9. **portal** (n.)

   a. _____

   b. _____

10. **trepidation** (n.)

   a. _____

   b. _____

Use the following list of synonyms and antonyms to fill in the blanks. Some of the words have no antonyms. In such cases, the antonym blanks have been marked with an X.

apprehension	door	kindly	rust	staid
bashfulness	dull	lustrous	showiness	stingy
cautiously	fortitude	polish	simply	uproarious
complexly	generous	recklessly	spiteful	wall

	Synonyms	**Antonyms**
1. **elaborately**	_____	_____
2. **boisterous**	_____	_____
3. **portal**	_____	_____
4. **luminous**	_____	_____
5. **flourish**	_____	_____
6. **burnish**	_____	_____
7. **gingerly**	_____	_____
8. **trepidation**	_____	_____
9. **benevolent**	_____	_____
10. **philanthropic**	_____	_____

Decide whether the first pair in the items below are synonyms or antonyms. Then choose the Master Word that shows a similar relation to the word(s) preceding the blank.

1. verify	:confirm	::entrance	: _____
2. attest	:protest	::plainly	: _____
3. noxious	:wholesome	::courage	: _____
4. calculation	:determination	::noisy	: _____
5. allay	:disturb	::carelessly	: _____
6. consumption	:tuberculosis	::charitable	: _____
7. formidable	:attractive	::cruel	: _____
8. subsequent	:future	::adornment	: _____
9. combustion	:explosion	::buff	: _____
10. inveigh	:praise	::faded	: _____

The Master Words in this lesson are repeated below. From the Master Words, choose the appropriate word for the blank in each of the following sentences. Write the word in the numbered space provided at the right.

benevolent	burnish	flourish	luminous	portal
boisterous	elaborately	gingerly	philanthropic	trepidation

1. On Saturday, he would sit in his room and ...?... the old trophies. 1. _____

2. Bullfighters always appear with (a, an) ...?... at the sound of fanfare and the cheers from the plaza. 2. _____

3. He ...?... picked up the injured bird and softly placed it in the basket. 3. _____

4. In the ancient years ...?... despots ruled with the iron fist in the velvet glove. 4. _____

5. The costumes were trimmed ...?... with sequins, lace, and velvet. 5. _____

6. The ...?... star flooded the calm lake with light. 6. _____

7. School lunch crowds may seem a bit ...?... to those who aren't accustomed to being around young people. 7. _____

8. The sign read: "Through this ...?... pass the world's most important people—our customers." 8. _____

9. Scrooge became ...?... and searched for acceptable ways to help others. 9. _____

10. With ...?... the defendant rose to hear the verdict. 10. _____

Fill in the chart below with the Master Word that fits each set of clues. Part of speech refers to the way the word is used in this lesson. Use a dictionary when necessary.

Number of Syllables	Part of Speech	Other Clues	Master Word
4	adjective	giving money to the arts, for example	1. _____
5	adverb	elegantly or intricately	2. _____
3	adjective	like loud partygoers	3. _____
2	noun	a fanfare, for example	4. _____
2	noun	a French door is one	5. _____
4	adjective	merciful and humane	6. _____
3	adjective	like a firefly	7. _____
4	noun	stage fright, for example	8. _____
3	adverb	how you walk on eggs	9. _____
2	verb	to apply lemon oil to furniture	10. _____

Read the following selection to get the general meaning. Read it a second time, paying special attention to the words in dark type. Notice how they are used in sentences. These are Master Words. These are the words you will be working with in this lesson.

From "Stratford on Avon"
by Washington Irving

I had come to Stratford on a poetical **pilgrimage.** My first visit was to the house where Shakespeare was born, and where, according to tradition, he was brought up to his father's craft of wool-combing. It is a small, mean-looking **edifice** of wood and plaster, a true nestling place of genius, which seems to delight in hatching its offspring in by-corners. The walls of its **squalid** chambers are covered with names and inscriptions in every language, by pilgrims of all nations, ranks, and conditions, from the prince to the peasant, and present a simple but striking instance of the **spontaneous** and universal **homage** of mankind to the great poet of nature.

The house is shown by a **garrulous** old lady, in a frosty red face, lighted up by a cold blue anxious eye, and **garnished** with artificial locks of flaxen hair, curling from under an exceedingly dirty cap. She was peculiarly **assiduous** in exhibiting the relics with which this, like all other celebrated shrines, abounds. There was the shattered stock of the very **matchlock** with which Shakespeare shot the deer on his poaching **exploits.**

EXERCISE 1

SELF-TEST: After reading the above selection, do the following. Look at the Master Words below. Underline the words that you think you know. Circle the words that you are less sure about. Draw a square around the words you don't recognize.

MASTER WORDS

assiduous	homage
edifice	matchlock
exploit	pilgrimage
garnished	spontaneous
garrulous	squalid

Read the selection on the preceding page again, this time paying special attention to the ten Master Words. In the (a) spaces provided below, write down what you think is the meaning of the word. After you have attempted a definition for each word, look up the word in a dictionary. In the (b) spaces, copy the appropriate dictionary definition.

1. **assiduous** (adj.)

    a. _____

    b. _____

2. **edifice** (n.)

    a. _____

    b. _____

3. **exploit** (n.)

    a. _____

    b. _____

4. **garnished** (adj.)

    a. _____

    b. _____

5. **garrulous** (adj.)

    a. _____

    b. _____

6. **homage** (n.)

    a. _____

    b. _____

7. **matchlock** (n.)

    a. _____

    b. _____

8. **pilgrimage** (n.)

    a. _____

    b. _____

9. **spontaneous** (adj.)

    a. _____

    b. _____

10. **squalid** (adj.)

    a. _____

    b. _____

Use the following list of synonyms and antonyms to fill in the blanks. Some words have no antonyms. In such cases, the antonym blanks have been marked with an X.

achievement	filthy	natural	talkative
building	gun	ramble	tidy
devotion	indolent	reticent	trimmed
diligent	inhibited	scorn	undecorated
failure	journey		

Synonyms   **Antonyms**

1. **pilgrimage**   _____   _____

2. **edifice**   _____   _____X_____

3. **matchlock**   _____   _____X_____

4. **squalid**   _____   _____

5. **spontaneous**   _____   _____

6. **homage**   _____   _____

7. **garrulous**   _____   _____

8. **garnished**   _____   _____

9. **assiduous**   _____   _____

10. **exploit**   _____   _____

Decide whether the first pair in the items below are synonyms or antonyms. Then choose the Master Word that shows a similar relation to the word(s) preceding the blank.

1. burnish   :shine   ::deed   : _____

2. luminous   :tarnished   ::restricted   : _____

3. philanthropic :humanitarian ::honor   : _____

4. boisterous   :disorderly   ::structure   : _____

5. elaborately :simply   ::unadorned   : _____

6. benevolent   :mean   ::lazy   : _____

7. flourish   :frill   ::musket   : _____

8. gingerly   :brashly   ::closemouthed : _____

9. portal   :entryway   ::trip   : _____

10. trepidation :boldness   ::neat   : _____

The Master Words in this lesson are repeated below. From the Master Words, choose the appropriate word for the blank in each of the following sentences. Write the word in the numbered space provided at the right.

assiduous	exploit	garrulous	matchlock	spontaneous
edifice	garnished	homage	pilgrimage	squalid

1. Each year thousands of Americans go to Arlington National Cemetery to pay ...?... to the Unknown Soldier.

   1. _____

2. *The Canterbury Tales* are told by Chaucer's fictional travellers on their ...?... to Canterbury.

   2. _____

3. The ...?...(s) of Ernest Hemingway as a hunter and fisherman are recounted in some of his stories and novels.

   3. _____

4. The cathedral is an imposing ...?... with a 300-foot spire.

   4. _____

5. Youngsters who live in ...?... surroundings are more likely to become victims of their environment.

   5. _____

6. The ...?... worker completed the job in one day.

   6. _____

7. Disc jockeys sometimes tend to be so ...?... that their programs are imbalanced between patter and music.

   7. _____

8. (A, An) ...?... demonstration broke out in the streets after news that the long war had finally come to a close.

   8. _____

9. I ordered a sandwich ...?... with tomato and lettuce.

   9. _____

10. The old ...?... turned out to be a valuable museum piece.

   10. _____

To complete the crossword, choose the Master Word associated with each word or phrase below. Begin each answer in the square having the same number as the clue.

1. this is paid on Memorial Day

2. the Taj Mahal is one

3. combustion might be this way

4. like a gourmet's cake

5. holy trek

6. a "pioneering" weapon

7. describes horrid living conditions

8. describes a wagging tongue

9. a hero's deed

10. describes one who strives for perfection

Read the following selection to get the general meaning. Read it a second time, paying special attention to the words in dark type. Notice how they are used in sentences. These are Master Words. These are the words you will be working with in this lesson.

From **"The Iron Shroud"**
by William Mudford

It was terrible to think of it! but it was yet more terrible to picture long, long years of captivity, in a solitude so **appalling,** a loneliness so dreary, that thought, for want of fellowship, would lose itself in madness or **stagnate** into idiocy.

He could not hope to escape, unless he had the power of **rending asunder,** with his bare hands, the solid iron walls of his prison. He could not hope for liberty from the **relenting** mercies of his enemy.

His instant death, under any form of refined cruelty, was not the object of Tolfi, for he might have **inflicted** it, and he had not. It was too evident, therefore, he was reserved for some **premeditated** scheme of **subtle** vengeance! and what vengeance could transcend in fiendish malice either the slow death of famine or the still slower one of solitary **incarceration,** till the last lingering spark of life **expired** or till reason fled, and nothing should remain to perish but the brute functions of the body?

EXERCISE 1

SELF-TEST: After reading the above selection, do the following. Look at the Master Words below. Underline the words that you think you know. Circle the words that you are less sure about. Draw a square around the words you don't recognize.

MASTER WORDS

appall	premeditated
asunder	relent
expire	rend
incarcerate	stagnate
inflict	subtle

Read the selection on the preceding page again, this time paying special attention to the ten Master Words. In the (a) spaces provided below, write down what you think is the meaning of the word. After you have attempted a definition for each word, look up the word in a dictionary. In the (b) spaces, copy the appropriate dictionary definition.

1. **appall** (v.)

   a. _____

   b. _____

2. **asunder** (adv.)

   a. _____

   b. _____

3. **expire** (v.)

   a. _____

   b. _____

4. **incarcerate** (v.)

   a. _____

   b. _____

5. **inflict** (v.)

   a. _____

   b. _____

6. **premeditated** (adj.)

   a. _____

   b. _____

7. **relent** (v.)

   a. _____

   b. _____

8. **rend** (v.)

   a. _____

   b. _____

9. **stagnate** (v.)

   a. _____

   b. _____

10. **subtle** (adj.)

    a. _____

    b. _____

Use the following list of synonyms and antonyms to fill in the blanks. Some words have no antonyms. In such cases, the antonym blanks have been marked with an X.

allure	horrify	penalize	soften
apart	imprison	perish	stitch
artful	intensify	predesigned	tear
flourish	languish	revive	together
heavy-handed	liberate	reward	unplanned

	Synonyms	**Antonyms**
1. **appall**	_____	_____
2. **stagnate**	_____	_____
3. **rend**	_____	_____
4. **asunder**	_____	_____
5. **relent**	_____	_____
6. **premeditated**	_____	_____
7. **subtle**	_____	_____
8. **incarcerate**	_____	_____
9. **expire**	_____	_____
10. **inflict**	_____	_____

Decide whether the first pair in the items below are synonyms or antonyms. Then choose the Master Word that shows a similar relation to the word(s) preceding the blank.

1. homage	:tribute	::impose	:	_____
2. assiduous	:idle	::renew	:	_____
3. pilgrimage	:tour	::decay	:	_____
4. garrulous	:silent	::unrehearsed	:	_____
5. matchlock	:flintlock	::split	:	_____
6. edifice	:building	::frighten	:	_____
7. exploit	:feat	::in pieces	:	_____
8. squalid	:clean	::obvious	:	_____
9. garnished	:plain	::release	:	_____
10. spontaneous	:restrained	::increase	:	_____

EXERCISE 5

The Master Words in this lesson are repeated below. From the Master Words, choose the appropriate word for the blank in each of the following sentences. Write the word in the numbered space provided at the right.

appall	expire	inflict	relent	stagnate
asunder	incarcerate	premeditated	rend	subtle

1. Daniel Defoe wrote some of his works while ...?...(d, ed) in a prison.

1. _____

2. The policy will ...?... 30 days after the date the premium is due.

2. _____

3. The worst earthquake in a century ...?...(d, ed) heavy casualties.

3. _____

4. There were ...?... differences in his color choices that went almost unnoticed unless you looked very hard.

4. _____

5. The mind, like the body, must have exercise or it will ...?... .

5. _____

6. Enemy tanks drove our army ...?... .

6. _____

7. Murderers are judged harshly, but most harshly when the murder is ...?... .

7. _____

8. The judge decided to ...?... and suspend the jail sentence.

8. _____

9. Stories of lingering death ...?... most people.

9. _____

10. The puppy will quickly ...?... the newspaper to shreds if given the chance.

10. _____

EXERCISE 6

The invented words below are formed from parts of different Master Words from this lesson. Create a definition and indicate the part of speech for each word. The first one is done for you.

premedirend   *(v.) to plan to separate in advance* _____

incarcerappall _____

premedexpire _____

subtlagnate _____

Now invent your own words by combining parts of the Master Words. Create a definition for each, and indicate the word's part of speech. (You may reuse any of the word parts above in new combinations.)

1. _____ _____

2. _____ _____

LESSON 24 Review of Lessons 13–23

PART I: From the list below, choose the correct word for each sentence that follows. Use each word only once.

assiduous	garnished	incarcerate	salutation
edifice	garrulous	martial	squalid
emulate	gingerly	peril	trepidation

1. The cat touched the water _____, not wanting to get her fur wet.

2. The thief was _____(d, ed) after he was caught with the diamonds.

3. The _____ young boy babbled on about the trip until his mother hushed him.

4. The hamburger was _____ with pickles.

5. Despite _____ practice, Paul failed to make the first team.

6. That _____ under construction will honor the earthquake victims.

7. The mountain climbers' lives were in _____ as they made the ascent up dangerous Mt. Hood.

8. The new recruits definitely lack a proper _____ bearing.

9. Those who live in _____ ghettos are deprived of the beauty of nature.

10. Marvin approached his parents with _____ after he received the speeding ticket.

11. Jim chose to _____ his hero's style and dress.

12. Our host's cool _____ did not make us feel welcome.

PART II: From the list below, choose the correct word for each sentence that follows. Use each word only once.

attest	metamorphosis	quell	surge
formidable	penury	reserved	verify
impervious	protract	speculate	vivid

1. Flood waters continue to _____ through the narrow streets, sweeping debris along the sidewalks.

2. The cause of Tom's _____ into a model student was never determined.

3. The engineer used a computer to _____ and cross-check his assistant's data.

4. The heavy snowstorm will _____ the project for two more weeks.

5. Expecting an easy victory, the visitors were surprised to find our team such (a, an) _____ opponent.

6. The detectives met to _____ about how the thieves entered the museum undetected.

7. My old-fashioned uncle is _____ to new ideas.

8. The attempts to _____ the riot and restore order were finally successful.

9. Sam had (a, an) _____ nightmare after watching the terrifying movie.

10. Our entire coaching staff will _____ to the effectiveness of Quik-Quench in restoring body fluids.

11. Though America is a wealthy nation, _____ still occurs in some parts of the country.

12. Mary's shy nature caused her to appear more _____ than she really was.

PART III: Decide whether the first pair in the items below are synonyms or antonyms. Then choose the Master Word from Lessons 13-23 which shows a similar relation to the word(s) preceding the blank. Do not repeat a Master Word that appears in the first column.

1. luminous	:vivid	::gloss	: _____
2. inflict	:administer	::end	: _____
3. garrulous	:chatty	::looting	: _____
4. expend	:conserve	::starve	: _____
5. rebuke	:compliment	::champion	: _____
6. trait	:distinction	::execute	: _____
7. peril	:danger	::proud	: _____
8. vexation	:pleasure	::disrespect	: _____
9. inveigh	:criticize	::definite	: _____
10. trepidation	:fear	::pigment	: _____
11. continual	:disconnected	::brutal	: _____
12. peculiar	:odd	::unrest	: _____
13. defunct	:extinct	::freedom	: _____
14. abuse	:injure	::irreverence	: _____
15. pensive	:thoughtful	::rowdy	: _____
16. severe	:hard	::wiggle	: _____
17. flourish	:simplicity	::trivial	: _____
18. stagnate	:regenerate	::sag	: _____
19. seize	:release	::unthreatening	: _____
20. spontaneous	:planned	::charm	: _____

Read the following selection to get the general meaning. Read it a second time, paying special attention to the words in dark type. Notice how they are used in sentences. These are Master Words. These are the words you will be working with in this lesson.

From **"The Two Drovers"**
by Sir Walter Scott

The horror of the bystanders began now to give way to **indignation;** and the sight of a favorite companion murdered in the midst of them, the **provocation** being, in their opinion, so utterly **inadequate** to the excess of vengeance, might have **induced** them to kill the perpetrator of the deed even upon the very spot. The constable, however, did his duty on this occasion, and, with the assistance of some of the more reasonable persons present, **procured** horses to guard the prisoner to Carlisle, to **abide** his doom at the next assizes. While the escort was preparing, the prisoner neither expressed the least interest nor attempted the slightest reply. Only before he was carried from the fatal apartment, he desired to look at the dead body, which, raised from the floor, had been deposited upon the large table (at the head of which Harry Wakefield had **presided** but a few minutes before, full of life, vigor and **animation**) until the surgeons should examine the mortal wound. The face of the corpse was decently covered with a napkin. To the surprise and horror of the bystanders, which displayed itself in a general *AH!* drawn through clenched teeth and half-shut lips, Robin Oig removed the cloth, and gazed with a mournful but steady eye on the lifeless **visage** which had been so lately animated, that the smile of good-humored confidence in his own strength, of conciliation at once, and contempt towards his enemy, still curled his lip. While those present expected that the wound, which had so lately flooded the apartment with **gore,** would send forth fresh streams at the touch of the homicide, Robin Oig replaced the covering, with the brief exclamation, "He was a pretty man!"

EXERCISE 1

SELF-TEST: After reading the above selection, do the following. Look at the Master Words below. Underline the words that you think you know. Circle the words that you are less sure about. Draw a square around the words you don't recognize.

MASTER WORDS

abide	induce
animation	preside
gore	procure
inadequate	provocation
indignation	visage

Read the selection on the preceding page again, this time paying special attention to the ten Master Words. In the (a) spaces provided below, write down what you think is the meaning of the word. After you have attempted a definition for each word, look up the word in a dictionary. In the (b) spaces, copy the appropriate dictionary definition.

1. **abide** (v.)

    a. _____

    b. _____

2. **animation** (n.)

    a. _____

    b. _____

3. **gore** (n.)

    a. _____

    b. _____

4. **inadequate** (adj.)

    a. _____

    b. _____

5. **indignation** (n.)

    a. _____

    b. _____

6. **induce** (v.)

    a. _____

    b. _____

7. **preside** (v.)

    a. _____

    b. _____

8. **procure** (v.)

    a. _____

    b. _____

9. **provocation** (n.)

    a. _____

    b. _____

10. **visage** (n.)

    a. _____

    b. _____

Use the following list of synonyms and antonyms to fill in the blanks. Some words have no antonyms. In such cases, the antonym blanks have been marked with an X.

anger	irritation	obtain	rebel
blood	lacking	oversee	stillness
discourage	mask	pacification	sufficient
distribute	movement	persuade	tolerate
face	neglect	pleasure	

	Synonyms	**Antonyms**
1. **indignation**	_____	_____
2. **provocation**	_____	_____
3. **induce**	_____	_____
4. **procure**	_____	_____
5. **abide**	_____	_____
6. **animation**	_____	_____
7. **visage**	_____	_____
8. **gore**	_____	X
9. **inadequate**	_____	_____
10. **preside**	_____	_____

Decide whether the first pair in the items below are synonyms or antonyms. Then choose the Master Word that shows a similar relation to the word(s) preceding the blank.

1. relent	:aggravate	::prevent	: _____
2. stagnate	:idle	::expression	: _____
3. appall	:terrify	::blood	: _____
4. asunder	:separately	::outrage	: _____
5. premeditated	:spontaneous	::plentiful	: _____
6. inflict	:force upon	::direct	: _____
7. subtle	:evident	::peacemaking	: _____
8. expire	:recharge	::revolt	: _____
9. rend	:rupture	::get	: _____
10. incarcerate	:unshackle	::inaction	: _____

The Master Words in this lesson are repeated below. From the Master Words, choose the appropriate word for the blank in each of the following sentences. Write the word in the numbered space provided at the right.

abide	gore	indignation	preside	provocation
animation	inadequate	induce	procure	visage

1. Shrewd advertisers can ...?... people to buy inferior products.   1. _____

2. Good speakers enhance their words with ...?... .   2. _____

3. Every teacher has to ...?... a certain amount of nonsense.   3. _____

4. Sensational newspapers report murders in detail, complete with all the ...?... .   4. _____

5. A display of righteous ...?... is most often justified if a teacher has exhausted all forms of correction.   5. _____

6. When both the president and vice-president fail to show up, the secretary should ...?... over the meeting.   6. _____

7. We can ...?... first-rate pottery at the Art Fair, but it will cost a lot more.   7. _____

8. The funds were ...?... to build a new auditorium.   8. _____

9. Countries, like people, will fight at the slightest ...?... .   9. _____

10. The ...?... (s) of the presidents were carved in the mountainside.   10. _____

Write the Master Word that is associated with each word group below. Then list three things that might be associated with the review word that follows.

1. insult, Pearl Harbor, dare   _____

2. medical advice, traffic laws, orders   _____

3. bullfight, slasher films, massacre   _____

4. lame excuse, below average, factory reject   _____

5. Mount Rushmore, mirror, makeup   _____

6. chairperson, judge, department head   _____

7. protest, resentment, offense   _____

8. dancer, gestures, lively discussions   _____

9. buyer, smuggler, recruiter   _____

10. lobbyist, brainwashing, commercials   _____

Review word: expire (Lesson 23)

_____   _____   _____

Read the following selection to get the general meaning. Read it a second time, paying special attention to the words in dark type. Notice how they are used in sentences. These are Master Words. These are the words you will be working with in this lesson.

From **"Sire de Malétroit's Door"**
by Robert Louis Stevenson

Denis cast a look around and darted into the porch. There he might escape observation, or—if that were too much to expect—was in a **capital** posture whether for **parley** or defense. So thinking, he drew his sword and tried to set his back against the door. To his surprise, it **yielded** behind his weight; and though he turned in a moment, continued to swing back on oiled and noiseless hinges, until it stood wide open on a black interior. When things fall out **opportunely** for the person concerned, he is not **apt** to be critical about the how or why, his own immediate personal convenience seeming a sufficient reason for the strangest oddities and revolutions in our **sublunary** things; and so Denis, without a moment's hesitation, stepped within and partly closed the door behind him to conceal his place of **refuge.** Nothing was further from his thoughts than to close it altogether; but for some **inexplicable** reason—perhaps by a spring or a weight—the **ponderous** mass of oak whipped itself out of his fingers and clanked to, with a formidable rumble and a noise like the falling of an **automatic** bar.

EXERCISE 1

SELF-TEST: After reading the above selection, do the following. Look at the Master Words below. Underline the words that you think you know. Circle the words that you are less sure about. Draw a square around the words you don't recognize.

MASTER WORDS

apt	**parley**
automatic	**ponderous**
capital	**refuge**
inexplicable	**sublunary**
opportunely	**yield**

Read the selection on the preceding page again, this time paying special attention to the ten Master Words. In the (a) spaces provided below, write down what you think is the meaning of the word. After you have attempted a definition for each word, look up the word in a dictionary. In the (b) spaces, copy the appropriate dictionary definition.

1. **apt** (adj.)

   a. _____

   b. _____

2. **automatic** (adj.)

   a. _____

   b. _____

3. **capital** (adj.)

   a. _____

   b. _____

4. **inexplicable** (adj.)

   a. _____

   b. _____

5. **opportunely** (adv.)

   a. _____

   b. _____

6. **parley** (n.)

   a. _____

   b. _____

7. **ponderous** (adj.)

   a. _____

   b. _____

8. **refuge** (n.)

   a. _____

   b. _____

9. **sublunary** (adj.)

   a. _____

   b. _____

10. **yield** (v.)

    a. _____

    b. _____

Use the following list of synonyms and antonyms to fill in the blanks. Some words have no antonyms. In such cases, the antonym blanks have been marked with an X.

belatedly	first-rate	massive	silence
clear	heavenly	petite	succumb
conference	inferior	resist	timely
earthly	likely	self-operating	unexplainable
exposure	manual	shelter	uninclined

	Synonyms	**Antonyms**
1. **capital**	_____	_____
2. **parley**	_____	_____
3. **yield**	_____	_____
4. **opportunely**	_____	_____
5. **apt**	_____	_____
6. **sublunary**	_____	_____
7. **refuge**	_____	_____
8. **inexplicable**	_____	_____
9. **ponderous**	_____	_____
10. **automatic**	_____	_____

Decide whether the first pair in the items below are synonyms or antonyms. Then choose the Master Word that shows a similar relation to the word(s) preceding the blank.

1. inadequate	:satisfactory	::poorly timed	: _____
2. induce	:hinder	::graceful	: _____
3. visage	:appearance	::worldly	: _____
4. procure	:gain	::asylum	: _____
5. provocation	:settlement	::withstand	: _____
6. abide	:resist	::unlikely	: _____
7. gore	:carnage	::excellent	: _____
8. indignation	:resentment	::push-button	: _____
9. animation	:motionlessness	::known	: _____
10. preside	:supervise	::discussion	: _____

EXERCISE 5

The Master Words in this lesson are repeated below. From the Master Words, choose the appropriate word for the blank in each of the following sentences. Write the word in the numbered space provided at the right.

| apt | capital | opportunely | ponderous | sublunary |
| automatic | inexplicable | parley | refuge | yield |

1. Some authors see humans as struggling against ...?... forces that determine their fate.

1. _____

2. He carried (a, an) ...?... book that weighed 35 pounds.

2. _____

3. Football players are ...?... to have strong legs.

3. _____

4. The winter birds sought ...?... near the feeder in the backyard.

4. _____

5. The three-day ...?... of the State Department officials was held in Paris.

5. _____

6. The principal said Richard was (a, an) ...?... Latin scholar and an even better Russian scholar.

6. _____

7. Churchill's famous speeches promised that the English would never ...?... to tyranny.

7. _____

8. ...?..., the sun shone for the first time in days as we started our "bike hike."

8. _____

9. Has the ...?... typewriter been replaced by the computer?

9. _____

10. ...?... experiences on earth seem inconsequential in terms of total activity in the universe.

10. _____

EXERCISE 6

To complete the word spiral, choose the Master Word associated with each phrase below. Start with 1 and fill in each answer clockwise. Be careful! Each new word may overlap the previous word by one or more letters.

1. what you seek in a storm

2. like baffling mysteries

3. at a convenient time

4. give up ground

5. an elephant or hippopotamus

6. down-to-earth

7. just liable to

8. a soda machine or traffic lights, for example

9. none better

10. serious dialogue

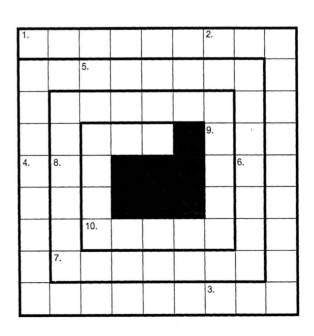

LESSON 27

Read the following selection to get the general meaning. Read it a second time, paying special attention to the words in dark type. Notice how they are used in sentences. These are Master Words. These are the words you will be working with in this lesson.

From "A Lodging for the Night"
by Robert Louis Stevenson

It was late in November, 1456. The snow fell over Paris with **rigorous,** relentless **persistence;** sometimes the wind made a sally and scattered it in flying **vortices;** sometimes there was a lull, and flake after flake descended out of the black night air, silent, **circuitous, interminable.** To poor people, looking up under moist eyebrows, it seemed a wonder where it all came from. Master Francis Villon had **propounded** an alternative that afternoon at a tavern window: was it only Pagan Jupiter plucking geese upon Olympus? or were the holy angels **molting?** He was only a poor Master of Arts, he went on; and as the question somewhat touched upon divinity, he durst not **venture** to conclude. A silly old priest from Montargis, who was among the company, treated the young rascal to a bottle of wine in honor of the jest and **grimaces** with which it was accompanied, and swore on his own white beard that he had been just such another **irreverent** dog when he was Villon's age.

The air was raw and pointed, but not far below freezing; and the flakes were large, damp, and adhesive. The whole city was sheeted up. An army might have marched from end to end and not a footfall given the alarm. If there were any belated birds in heaven, they saw the island like a large white patch, and the bridges like slim white spars, on the black ground of the river.

EXERCISE 1

SELF-TEST: After reading the above selection, do the following. Look at the Master Words below. Underline the words that you think you know. Circle the words that you are less sure about. Draw a square around the words you don't recognize.

MASTER WORDS

circuitous	persistence
grimace	propound
interminable	rigorous
irreverent	venture
molt	vortex

Read the selection on the preceding page again, this time paying special attention to the ten Master Words. In the (a) spaces provided below, write down what you think is the meaning of the word. After you have attempted a definition for each word, look up the word in a dictionary. In the (b) spaces, copy the appropriate dictionary definition.

1. **circuitous** (adj.)

   a. _____

   b. _____

2. **grimace** (n.)

   a. _____

   b. _____

3. **interminable** (adj.)

   a. _____

   b. _____

4. **irreverent** (adj.)

   a. _____

   b. _____

5. **molt** (v.)

   a. _____

   b. _____

6. **persistence** (n.)

   a. _____

   b. _____

7. **propound** (v.)

   a. _____

   b. _____

8. **rigorous** (adj.)

   a. _____

   b. _____

9. **venture** (v.)

   a. _____

   b. _____

10. **vortex** (n.)

   a. _____

   b. _____

Use the following list of synonyms and antonyms to fill in the blanks. Some words have no antonyms. In such cases, the antonym blanks have been marked with an X.

abandon	finite	respectful	straight
attempt	frown	severe	suggest
calm	heretical	shed	surrender
conceal	indirect	smile	unceasing
feather	perseverance	soft	whirl

	Synonyms	**Antonyms**
1. **rigorous**	_____	_____
2. **persistence**	_____	_____
3. **irreverent**	_____	_____
4. **vortex**	_____	_____
5. **circuitous**	_____	_____
6. **interminable**	_____	_____
7. **propound**	_____	_____
8. **molt**	_____	_____
9. **venture**	_____	_____
10. **grimace**	_____	_____

Decide whether the first pair in the items below are synonyms or antonyms. Then choose the Master Word that shows a similar relation to the word(s) preceding the blank.

1. automatic	:spontaneous	::discard	: _____
2. refuge	:safety	::risk	: _____
3. capital	:first-class	::scowl	: _____
4. parley	:talk	::offer	: _____
5. opportunely	:unfavorably	::submission	: _____
6. apt	:doubtful	::direct	: _____
7. yield	:challenge	::sincere	: _____
8. inexplicable	:certain	::measurable	: _____
9. sublunary	:mundane	::eddy	: _____
10. ponderous	:dainty	::mild	: _____

The Master Words in this lesson are repeated below. From the Master Words, choose the appropriate word for the blank in each of the following sentences. Write the word in the numbered space provided at the right.

circuitous	interminable	molt	propound	venture
grimace	irreverent	persistence	rigorous	vortex

1. One glance at the lengthy tax form brought (a, an) ...?... to his face.

1. _____

2. A successful financial ...?... usually involves some risk along the way.

2. _____

3. We followed (a, an) ...?... path around the mountain.

3. _____

4. The ...?... of the storm churned, and the great tail of the tornado swept the land barren.

4. _____

5. ...?... in reaching a goal can make up for a shortage of talent.

5. _____

6. This administration's economists ...?... the theory that the country should be financed by a single tax on property.

6. _____

7. Animals ...?... at certain times of the year.

7. _____

8. If you have been separated from one dear to you, the moments until reunion seem ...?... .

8. _____

9. Their physical fitness routine is short but very ...?... .

9. _____

10. Horseplay in church is considered ...?... .

10. _____

Use at least five Master Words from this lesson to write a scene about one of the following topics. Or create a topic of your own. Write your choice on the blank. Circle the Master Words as you use them.

Possible Topics: The Long Lecture, The Obstacle Course

_____

_____

_____

_____

_____

_____

_____

_____

LESSON 28

Read the following selection to get the general meaning. Read it a second time, paying special attention to the words in dark type. Notice how they are used in sentences. These are Master Words. These are the words you will be working with in this lesson.

From "The Three Strangers"
by Thomas Hardy

When this was done, and the man had gone his way, the night was found to be so far advanced that it was deemed useless to renew the search before the next morning.

Next day, accordingly, the **quest** for the clever sheep-stealer became general and **keen,** to all appearance at least. But the intended punishment was cruelly **disproportioned** to the **transgression,** and the sympathy of a great many country-folk in that district was strongly on the side of the **fugitive.** Moreover, his marvelous coolness and daring in hob-and-nobbing with the hangman, under the **unprecedented** circumstances of the shepherd's party, won their admiration. So that it may be questioned if all those who **ostensibly** made themselves so busy in exploring woods and fields and lanes were quite so thorough when it came to the private examination of their own lofts and buildings. Stories were afloat of a mysterious figure being occasionally seen in some old overgrown trackway or other, **remote** from turnpike roads, but when a search was **instituted** in any of these suspected quarters, nobody was found. Thus the days and weeks passed without **tidings.**

In brief, the bass-voiced man of the chimney corner was never recaptured. Some said that he went across the sea, others that he did not, but buried himself in the depths of a populous city.

EXERCISE 1

SELF-TEST: After reading the above selection, do the following. Look at the Master Words below. Underline the words that you think you know. Circle the words that you are less sure about. Draw a square around the words you don't recognize.

MASTER WORDS

disproportion	**quest**
fugitive	**remote**
institute	**tidings**
keen	**transgression**
ostensibly	**unprecedented**

Read the selection on the preceding page again, this time paying special attention to the ten Master Words. In the (a) spaces provided below, write down what you think is the meaning of the word. After you have attempted a definition for each word, look up the word in a dictionary. In the (b) spaces, copy the appropriate dictionary definition.

1. **disproportion** (v.)

   a. _____

   b. _____

2. **fugitive** (n.)

   a. _____

   b. _____

3. **institute** (v.)

   a. _____

   b. _____

4. **keen** (adj.)

   a. _____

   b. _____

5. **ostensibly** (adv.)

   a. _____

   b. _____

6. **quest** (n.)

   a. _____

   b. _____

7. **remote** (adj.)

   a. _____

   b. _____

8. **tidings** (n.)

   a. _____

   b. _____

9. **transgression** (n.)

   a. _____

   b. _____

10. **unprecedented** (adj.)

   a. _____

   b. _____

Use the following list of synonyms and antonyms to fill in the blanks. Some words have no antonyms. In such cases, the antonym blanks have been marked with an X.

apparently	distant	indifferent	really
atonement	enthusiastic	misdeed	search
balance	escapee	mismatch	secrecy
commence	halt	near	unique
commonplace	hunter	news	

	Synonyms	**Antonyms**
1. **quest**	_____	X _____
2. **keen**	_____	_____
3. **disproportion**	_____	_____
4. **transgression**	_____	_____
5. **fugitive**	_____	_____
6. **unprecedented**	_____	_____
7. **ostensibly**	_____	_____
8. **remote**	_____	_____
9. **institute**	_____	_____
10. **tidings**	_____	_____

Decide whether the first pair in the items below are synonyms or antonyms. Then choose the Master Word that shows a similar relation to the word(s) preceding the blank.

1. vortex	:whirlpool	::information	:	_____
2. molt	:shed	::seemingly	:	_____
3. grimace	:glare	::runaway	:	_____
4. circuitous	:unswerving	::equalize	:	_____
5. propound	:propose	::start	:	_____
6. irreverent	:heartfelt	::ordinary	:	_____
7. venture	:chance	::hunt	:	_____
8. rigorous	:easy	::good deed	:	_____
9. persistence	:yielding	::close	:	_____
10. interminable	:definite	::unexcited	:	_____

The Master Words in this lesson are repeated below. From the Master Words, choose the appropriate word for the blank in each of the following sentences. Write the word in the numbered space provided at the right.

| disproportion | institute | ostensibly | remote | transgression |
| fugitive | keen | quest | tidings | unprecedented |

1. The ancient Greeks frequently killed the messenger who brought bad ...?... .

1. _____

2. President Franklin D. Roosevelt shocked some voters when he announced he would try for (a, an) ...?... third term.

2. _____

3. The reforms were ...?...(d, ed) under the old administration but carried out by those now in power.

3. _____

4. Kurtz lived in (a, an) ...?... section of unexplored jungle.

4. _____

5. The scientists' ...?... for knowledge is neverending.

5. _____

6. The English are very ...?... on soccer and crossword puzzles.

6. _____

7. The judge vowed he would never willingly or consciously ...?... prisoners' sentences.

7. _____

8. The ...?... gave up and turned herself in.

8. _____

9. ...?... he was ill and had to go home, but we suspect there was another reason.

9. _____

10. Some ...?...(s) of traffic laws go undetected because of inadequate police forces.

10. _____

Fill in the chart below with the Master Word that fits each set of clues. Part of speech refers to the word's usage in the lesson. Use the glossary when necessary.

Number of Syllables	Part of Speech	Other Clues	Master Word
2	adjective	farther than a stone's throw	1. _____
3	noun	sin or felony	2. _____
2	noun	good news or bad	3. _____
3	verb	establish a new system, for example	4. _____
4	adverb	how it appears to be	5. _____
5	adjective	hasn't happened before	6. _____
4	verb	to throw out of kilter	7. _____
1	noun	the search for the Holy Grail, for instance	8. _____
1	adjective	gung-ho	9. _____
3	noun	outlaw or gangster, maybe	10. _____

Read the following selection to get the general meaning. Read it a second time, paying special attention to the words in dark type. Notice how they are used in sentences. These are Master Words. These are the words you will be working with in this lesson.

From **The Red Badge of Courage**
by Stephen Crane

His fingers **twined** nervously about his rifle. He wished that it was an engine of **annihilating** power. He felt that he and his companions were being taunted and **derided** from sincere **convictions** that they were poor and **puny.** His knowledge of his inability to take vengeance for it made his rage into a dark and stormy **specter,** that possessed him and made him dream of **abominable** cruelties. The tormentors were flies sucking **insolently** at his blood, and he thought that he would have given his life for a **revenge** of seeing their faces in pitiful plights.

When, in a dream, it occurred to the youth that his rifle was an **impotent** stick, he lost sense of everything but his hate, his desire to smash into pulp the glittering smile of victory which he could feel upon the faces of his enemies.

The blue smoke-swallowed line curled and writhed like a snake stepped upon. It swung its ends to and fro in an agony of fear and rage.

EXERCISE 1

SELF-TEST: After reading the above selection, do the following. Look at the Master Words below. Underline the words that you think you know. Circle the words that you are less sure about. Draw a square around the words you don't recognize.

MASTER WORDS

abominable	insolent
annihilate	puny
conviction	revenge
deride	specter
impotent	twine

Read the selection on the preceding page again, this time paying special attention to the ten Master Words. In the (a) spaces provided below, write down what you think is the meaning of the word. After you have attempted a definition for each word, look up the word in a dictionary. In the (b) spaces, copy the appropriate dictionary definition.

1. **abominable** (adj.)

    a. _____

    b. _____

2. **annihilate** (v.)

    a. _____

    b. _____

3. **conviction** (n.)

    a. _____

    b. _____

4. **deride** (v.)

    a. _____

    b. _____

5. **impotent** (adj.)

    a. _____

    b. _____

6. **insolent** (adj.)

    a. _____

    b. _____

7. **puny** (adj.)

    a. _____

    b. _____

8. **revenge** (n.)

    a. _____

    b. _____

9. **specter** (n.)

    a. _____

    b. _____

10. **twine** (v.)

    a. _____

    b. _____

Use the following list of synonyms and antonyms to fill in the blanks. Some words have no antonyms. In such cases, the antonym blanks have been marked with an X.

apparition	esteem	lovable	restore
belief	forgiveness	mock	strong
demolish	impertinent	reality	stunted
detestable	ineffective	reprisal	twist
doubt	large	respectful	untangle

	Synonyms	**Antonyms**
1. **twine**	_____	_____
2. **annihilate**	_____	_____
3. **deride**	_____	_____
4. **conviction**	_____	_____
5. **puny**	_____	_____
6. **specter**	_____	_____
7. **abominable**	_____	_____
8. **insolent**	_____	_____
9. **revenge**	_____	_____
10. **impotent**	_____	_____

Decide whether the first pair in the items below are synonyms or antonyms. Then choose the Master Word that shows a similar relation to the word(s) preceding the blank.

1. keen	:cool	::polite	: _____
2. institute	:bring about	::commitment	: _____
3. remote	:nearby	::forceful	: _____
4. ostensibly	:evidently	::destroy	: _____
5. transgression	:amends	::sturdy	: _____
6. quest	:pursuit	::ghost	: _____
7. disproportion	:balance	::praise	: _____
8. tidings	:news	::wind	: _____
9. fugitive	:refugee	::hateful	: _____
10. unprecedented	:usual	::mercy	: _____

The Master Words in this lesson are repeated below. From the Master Words, choose the appropriate word for the blank in each of the following sentences. Write the word in the numbered space provided at the right.

abominable	conviction	impotent	puny	specter
annihilate	deride	insolent	revenge	twine

1. Atomic bombs could ...?... all of humanity.

1. _____

2. The ...?... of famine haunts many overpopulated nations.

2. _____

3. (A, An) ...?... answer is not likely to gain you many favors.

3. _____

4. Our team batting average sagged to .210, thanks to the ...?... performance of our once big hitters.

4. _____

5. The ...?... plague swept London in the early 17th century.

5. _____

6. He was not the most popular senator, mainly because he voted his ...?...(s) rather than attempting to please others.

6. _____

7. Dale was (a, an) ...?... boy whose growth had been interrupted by a long childhood illness.

7. _____

8. Fans like to ...?... players who are not doing well, often jeering and booing.

8. _____

9. In the second fight, the old champ got his ...?..., whipping the newcomer in 10 rounds.

9. _____

10. Rambling branches ...?... about the rocks and through the gorge.

10. _____

Use at least five Master Words from this lesson to write a scene about one of the following topics. Or create a topic of your own. Write your choice on the blank. Circle the Master Words as you use them.

Possible Topics: A Dare, The Haunted House

_____

_____

_____

_____

_____

_____

_____

_____

Read the following selection to get the general meaning. Read it a second time, paying special attention to the words in dark type. Notice how they are used in sentences. These are Master Words. These are the words you will be working with in this lesson.

From "Sinners in the Hands of an Angry God" by Jonathan Edwards

The **wrath** of God is like great waters that are dammed for the present; they increase more and more and rise higher and higher, till an outlet is given; and the longer the stream is stopped, the more rapid and mighty is its course when once it is let loose. 'Tis true that judgment against your evil work has not been **executed** hitherto; the floods of God's **vengeance** have been withheld; but your guilt in the meantime is constantly increasing, and you are every day treasuring up more wrath; the waters are continually rising and **waxing** more and more mighty; and there is nothing but the **mere** pleasure of God that holds the waters back, that are unwilling to be stopped, and press hard to go forward. If God should only withdraw his hand from the floodgate it would immediately fly open, and the fiery floods of the fierceness and wrath of God would rush forth with **inconceivable** fury, and would come upon you with **omnipotent** power; and if your strength were ten thousand times greater than it is, yea, ten thousand times greater than the strength of the stoutest, **sturdiest** devil in hell, it would be nothing to withstand or **endure** it.

The bow of God's wrath is bent, and the arrow made ready on the string, and justice bends the arrow at your heart and strains the bow, and it is nothing but the mere pleasure of God, and that of an angry God, without any promise or **obligation** at all, that keeps the arrow one moment from being made drunk with your blood.

EXERCISE 1

SELF-TEST: After reading the above selection, do the following. Look at the Master Words below. Underline the words that you think you know. Circle the words that you are less sure about. Draw a square around the words you don't recognize.

MASTER WORDS

endure	omnipotent
execute	sturdy
inconceivable	vengeance
mere	wax
obligation	wrath

Read the selection on the preceding page again, this time paying special attention to the ten Master Words. In the (a) spaces provided below, write down what you think is the meaning of the word. After you have attempted a definition for each word, look up the word in a dictionary. In the (b) spaces, copy the appropriate dictionary definition.

1. **endure** (v.)

   a. _____

   b. _____

2. **execute** (v.)

   a. _____

   b. _____

3. **inconceivable** (adj.)

   a. _____

   b. _____

4. **mere** (adj.)

   a. _____

   b. _____

5. **obligation** (adj.)

   a. _____

   b. _____

6. **omnipotent** (adj.)

   a. _____

   b. _____

7. **sturdy** (adj.)

   a. _____

   b. _____

8. **vengeance** (n.)

   a. _____

   b. _____

9. **wax** (v.)

   a. _____

   b. _____

10. **wrath** (n.)

   a. _____

   b. _____

Use the following list of synonyms and antonyms to fill in the blanks. Some words have no antonyms. In such cases, the antonym blanks have been marked with an X.

all-powerful	grow	possible	solvency
debt	impotent	retribution	unimaginable
forgiveness	malinger	robust	wane
fragile	many	serenity	withstand
fury	perform	sole	yield

	Synonyms	**Antonyms**
1. **wrath**	_____	_____
2. **execute**	_____	_____
3. **vengeance**	_____	_____
4. **wax**	_____	_____
5. **inconceivable**	_____	_____
6. **mere**	_____	_____
7. **omnipotent**	_____	_____
8. **sturdy**	_____	_____
9. **endure**	_____	_____
10. **obligation**	_____	_____

Decide whether the first pair in the items below are synonyms or antonyms. Then choose the Master Word that shows a similar relation to the word(s) preceding the blank.

1. abominable	:horrid	::carry out	: _____
2. revenge	:pardon	::calmness	: _____
3. conviction	:principle	::duty	: _____
4. deride	:applaud	::resign	: _____
5. impotent	:powerful	::helpless	: _____
6. annihilate	:massacre	::only	: _____
7. specter	:spirit	::revenge	: _____
8. puny	:muscular	::weak	: _____
9. twine	:braid	::increase	: _____
10. insolent	:worshipful	::understandable	: _____

The Master Words in this lesson are repeated below. From the Master Words, choose the appropriate word for the blank in each of the following sentences. Write the word in the numbered space provided at the right.

endure	inconceivable	obligation	sturdy	wax
execute	mere	omnipotent	vengeance	wrath

1. Believing "a soft answer turneth away ...?..." may help keep the peace.

   1. _____

2. Martin was slow in paying off his ...?... to his generous hosts.

   2. _____

3. His business grew fast and seemed to ...?... even more prosperously after he hired an advertising manager.

   3. _____

4. Most economists find it ...?... that people can be hungry in a nation of so much wealth.

   4. _____

5. With all the activity in the children's room, we decided to put the ...?... old chairs in there.

   5. _____

6. Cancer patients may ...?... great pain during their illness.

   6. _____

7. After receiving instruction in swimming, the real test is your ability to ...?... the skills.

   7. _____

8. The old man plotted ...?... against his son's murderer.

   8. _____

9. Although a computer is a wonderful instrument, it is not ...?... and cannot do everything as many believe.

   9. _____

10. Happy workers do not feel like ...?... pawns on a chess board.

   10. _____

Write the Master Word that is associated with each word group below. Then list three things that might be associated with the review word that follows.

1. the Creator, total dictator, Superman

   _____

2. mountain goat, weight lifter, hiking boots

   _____

3. orders, a will, a plan

   _____

4. moon, crops, population

   _____

5. violence, Judgment Day, bad blood

   _____

6. immortality, nothingness, infinity

   _____

7. harsh weather, suffering, hardship

   _____

8. vendetta, lynch mob, feud

   _____

9. simple, sheer, downright

   _____

10. loan, contract, pledge

   _____

Review word: specter (Lesson 29)

_____   _____   _____

Read the following selection to get the general meaning. Read it a second time, paying special attention to the words in dark type. Notice how they are used in sentences. These are Master Words. These are the words you will be working with in this lesson.

From "The Marionettes"
by O. Henry

A man, wearing a long overcoat, with his hat tilted down in front, and carrying something in one hand, walked softly but rapidly out of the black alley. The policeman **accosted** him **civilly,** but with the assured air that is linked with **conscious** authority. The hour, the alley's musty reputation, the pedestrian's haste, the burden he carried—these easily combined into the "suspicious circumstances" that required **illumination** at the officer's hands.

The "suspect" halted readily and tilted back his hat, **exposing,** in the flicker of the electric lights, an emotionless, smooth countenance with a rather long nose and steady dark eyes. Thrusting his gloved hand into a side pocket of his overcoat, he drew out a card, and handed it to the policeman. Holding it to catch the uncertain light, the officer read the name "Charles Spencer James, M.D." The street and number of the address were of a neighborhood so solid and respectable as to subdue even curiosity. The policeman's downward glance at the article carried in the doctor's hand—a handsome medicine case of black leather, with small silver mountings—further **endorsed** the guarantee of the card.

"All right, doctor," said the officer, stepping aside, with an air of bulky **affability.** "Orders are to be extra careful. Good many burglars and holdups lately. Bad night to be out. Not so cold, but—clammy."

With a formal inclination of his head, and a word or two **corroborative** of the officer's estimate of the weather, Doctor James continued his somewhat rapid progress. Three times that night had a patrolman accepted his professional card and the sight of his **paragon** of a medicine case as **vouchers** for his honesty of person and purpose.

EXERCISE 1

SELF-TEST: After reading the above selection, do the following. Look at the Master Words below. Underline the words that you think you know. Circle the words that you are less sure about. Draw a square around the words you don't recognize.

MASTER WORDS

accost	endorse
affability	expose
civil	illumination
conscious	paragon
corroborate	voucher

Read the selection on the preceding page again, this time paying special attention to the ten Master Words. In the (a) spaces provided below, write down what you think is the meaning of the word. After you have attempted a definition for each word, look up the word in a dictionary. In the (b) spaces, copy the appropriate dictionary definition.

1. **accost** (v.)

   a. _____

   b. _____

2. **affability** (n.)

   a. _____

   b. _____

3. **civil** (adj.)

   a. _____

   b. _____

4. **conscious** (adj.)

   a. _____

   b. _____

5. **corroborate** (v.)

   a. _____

   b. _____

6. **endorse** (v.)

   a. _____

   b. _____

7. **expose** (v.)

   a. _____

   b. _____

8. **illumination** (n.)

   a. _____

   b. _____

9. **paragon** (n.)

   a. _____

   b. _____

10. **voucher** (n.)

   a. _____

   b. _____

Use the following list of synonyms and antonyms to fill in the blanks. Some words have no antonyms. In such cases, the antonym blanks have been marked with an X.

approve	disclaimer	hostility	pariah
aware	enlightenment	ignorant	receipt
bare	friendliness	ignore	reject
confirm	greet	model	repudiate
courteous	hide	obscurity	rude

	Synonyms	**Antonyms**
1. **accost**	_____	_____
2. **conscious**	_____	_____
3. **illumination**	_____	_____
4. **expose**	_____	_____
5. **endorse**	_____	_____
6. **corroborate**	_____	_____
7. **paragon**	_____	_____
8. **voucher**	_____	_____
9. **affability**	_____	_____
10. **civil**	_____	_____

Decide whether the first pair in the items below are synonyms or antonyms. Then choose the Master Word that shows a similar relation to the word(s) preceding the blank.

1. sturdy	:feeble	::refuse	: _____
2. mere	:bare	::support	: _____
3. wrath	:peace	::conceal	: _____
4. execute	:achieve	::confront	: _____
5. vengeance	:punishment	::perfect example	: _____
6. inconceivable	:believable	::bad-mannered	: _____
7. obligation	:requirement	::insight	: _____
8. endure	:surrender	::unfriendliness	: _____
9. wax	:expand	::proof	: _____
10. omnipotent	:powerless	::unaware	: _____

The Master Words in this lesson are repeated below. From the Master Words, choose the appropriate word for the blank in each of the following sentences. Write the word in the numbered space provided at the right.

accost	civil	corroborate	expose	paragon
affability	conscious	endorse	illumination	voucher

1. Few people are ...?... of their most annoying mannerisms.   1. _____

2. Newspapers should ...?... incidents of graft in public office.   2. _____

3. Newspapers may ...?... a candidate on the editorial page.   3. _____

4. This ...?... must be presented to receive the tickets.   4. _____

5. ...?... is a trait that salespeople should possess.   5. _____

6. People who do not always agree can at least be ...?... to one another.   6. _____

7. Everyone believed the witness, but we could not find another witness to ...?... his testimony.   7. _____

8. Department stores have found that ...?... in doorways and parking lots cuts down burglary.   8. _____

9. The smugness of (a, an) ...?... of virtue is the least virtuous thing of all.   9. _____

10. Panhandlers are likely to ...?... you on street corners of cities.   10. _____

Order the words in each item from *least* to *most.* Use the abbreviations *L* for "least" and *M* for "most." Leave the line before the word of the middle degree blank. The first word provides a clue about how to arrange the words. See the example.

effort: ____endeavor   _M_overexert   _L_loaf
(*Loaf* indicates the least effort; *overexert* indicates the most effort.)

1. verified: ____prove   ____claim   ____corroborate

2. rude: ____impolite   ____civil   ____gallant

3. informed: ____investigation   ____illumination   ____confusion

4. hostile: ____accost   ____welcome   ____snub

5. aware: ____absentminded   ____oblivious   ____conscious

6. jolly: ____affability   ____gloominess   ____merrymaking

7. excellent: ____paragon   ____noteworthy   ____adequate

8. hidden: ____expose   ____conceal   ____shade

9. approved: ____consider   ____protest   ____endorse

10. positive: ____voucher   ____denial   ____support

Read the following selection to get the general meaning. Read it a second time, paying special attention to the words in dark type. Notice how they are used in sentences. These are Master Words. These are the words you will be working with in this lesson.

From **"The Furnished Room"**
by O. Henry

One by one, as the characters of a cryptograph become explicit, the little signs left by the furnished room's procession of guests developed a significance. The threadbare space in the rug in front of the dresser told that lovely women had marched in the throng. Tiny fingerprints on the wall spoke of little prisoners trying to feel their way to sun and air. A splattered stain, raying like the shadow of a bursting bomb, witnessed where a hurled glass or bottle had splintered with its contents against the wall. Across the pier glass had been scrawled with a diamond in staggering letters the name "Marie." It seemed that the succession of dwellers in the furnished room had turned in fury—perhaps tempted beyond **forbearance** by its **garish** coldness—and wreaked upon it their passions. The furniture was chipped and bruised; the couch, distorted by bursting springs, seemed a horrible monster that had been slain during the **stress** of some **grotesque convulsion.** Some more **potent** upheaval had **cloven** a great slice from the marble mantel. Each plank in the floor owned its particular cant and shriek as from a separate and individual agony. It seemed **incredible** that all this **malice** and injury had been wrought upon the room by those who had called it for a time their home; and yet it may have been the cheated home instinct surviving blindly, the **resentful** rage at false household gods that had kindled their wrath. A hut that is our own we can sweep and adorn and cherish.

EXERCISE 1

SELF-TEST: After reading the above selection, do the following. Look at the Master Words below. Underline the words that you think you know. Circle the words that you are less sure about. Draw a square around the words you don't recognize.

MASTER WORDS

cleave	incredible
convulsion	malice
forbearance	potent
garish	resentful
grotesque	stress

Read the selection on the preceding page again, this time paying special attention to the ten Master Words. In the (a) spaces provided below, write down what you think is the meaning of the word. After you have attempted a definition for each word, look up the word in a dictionary. In the (b) spaces, copy the appropriate dictionary definition.

1. **cleave** (v.)

    a. _____

    b. _____

2. **convulsion** (n.)

    a. _____

    b. _____

3. **forbearance** (n.)

    a. _____

    b. _____

4. **garish** (adj.)

    a. _____

    b. _____

5. **grotesque** (adj.)

    a. _____

    b. _____

6. **incredible** (adj.)

    a. _____

    b. _____

7. **malice** (n.)

    a. _____

    b. _____

8. **potent** (adj.)

    a. _____

    b. _____

9. **resentful** (adj.)

    a. _____

    b. _____

10. **stress** (n.)

    a. _____

    b. _____

Use the following list of synonyms and antonyms to fill in the blanks. Some words have no antonyms. In such cases, the antonym blanks have been marked with an X.

benign	goodwill	plain	restraint
bitter	indulgence	plausible	spasm
bizarre	ineffectual	pressure	spite
charming	join	quiescence	split
gaudy	mighty	relaxation	unbelievable

Synonyms **Antonyms**

1. **forbearance** _____ _____

2. **garish** _____ _____

3. **malice** _____ _____

4. **stress** _____ _____

5. **grotesque** _____ _____

6. **convulsion** _____ _____

7. **potent** _____ _____

8. **cleave** _____ _____

9. **incredible** _____ _____

10. **resentful** _____ _____

Decide whether the first pair in the items below are synonyms or antonyms. Then choose the Master Word that shows a similar relation to the word(s) preceding the blank.

1. illumination :awareness ::deformed : _____

2. accost :approach ::sever : _____

3. affability :ill will ::excess : _____

4. endorse :veto ::powerless : _____

5. conscious :unknowing ::believable : _____

6. civil :disagreeable ::tasteful : _____

7. voucher :acknowledgment ::tension : _____

8. paragon :ideal ::hostile : _____

9. expose :disguise ::sympathy : _____

10. corroborate :verify ::disturbance : _____

The Master Words in this lesson are repeated below. From the Master Words, choose the appropriate word for the blank in each of the following sentences. Write the word in the numbered space provided at the right.

cleave	forbearance	grotesque	malice	resentful
convulsion	garish	incredible	potent	stress

1. Job interviews are frequently designed to put applicants under great ...?..., thus showing how they withstand pressure.

    1. _____

2. The great Casey had (a, an) ...?... bat; nevertheless, he struck out.

    2. _____

3. Horror movies are often filled with ...?... characters.

    3. _____

4. No nation escapes the ...?... of war, and the upheaval continues into the peaceful years that may follow.

    4. _____

5. Officials heard (a, an) ...?... tale from the man who saw the UFO.

    5. _____

6. Some nations are understandably ...?... toward countries that are richer and stronger.

    6. _____

7. It took great ...?... on my part not to react in anger.

    7. _____

8. Lincoln said we should conclude rivalries and hold "...?... toward none."

    8. _____

9. Meat cutters ...?... beef quarters into choice portions.

    9. _____

10. Cheap jewelry frequently creates (a, an) ...?..., overdressed look.

    10. _____

To complete this puzzle, fill in the Master Word associated with each phrase below. Then unscramble the circled letters to form a Master Word from Lesson 31, and define it.

1. amazing and awesome

    — — — Ⓞ — — — — — —

2. keeping silent or dieting are examples

    — — — — — — — — — Ⓞ —

3. Frankenstein's monster

    — — — — — — — — Ⓞ —

4. chop wood, for example

    — — — — — —

5. tacky and "loud"

    — — — — — Ⓞ

6. uncontrolled laughter, for example

    — — Ⓞ — — — — — —

7. what enemies feel toward each other

    — — — — Ⓞ —

8. you might experience this before an exam

    — — — — — —

9. bitter or injured

    — Ⓞ — — — — — — —

10. TNT or words are this

    — Ⓞ — — — — —

Unscrambled word: _____

Definition: _____

Read the following selection to get the general meaning. Read it a second time, paying special attention to the words in dark type. Notice how they are used in sentences. These are Master Words. These are the words you will be working with in this lesson.

From **"The Furnished Room"**
by O. Henry

The young **tenant** in the chair allowed these thoughts to file, soft-shod, through his mind, while there drifted into the room furnished sounds and furnished scents. He heard in one room a tittering and incontinent, slack laughter; in others the **monologue** of a scold, the rattling of dice, a lullaby, and one crying dully; above him a banjo tinkled with spirit. Doors banged somewhere; the elevated trains roared **intermittently;** a cat yowled miserably upon a back fence. And he breathed the breath of the house—a **dank savor** rather than a smell—a cold, musty effluvium [vapor] as from underground vaults **mingled** with the **reeking** exhalations of linoleum and mildewed and rotten woodwork.

Then suddenly, as he rested there, the room was filled with the strong, sweet odor of mignonette [a fragrant flower]. It came as upon a single **buffet** of wind with such sureness and fragrance and emphasis that it almost seemed a living **visitant.** And the man cried aloud: "What, dear?" as if he had been called, and sprang up and faced about. The rich odor clung to him and wrapped him around. He reached out his arms for it, all his senses for the time confused and commingled. How could one be **peremptorily** called by an odor? Surely it must have been a sound.

EXERCISE 1

SELF-TEST: After reading the above selection, do the following. Look at the Master Words below. Underline the words that you think you know. Circle the words that you are less sure about. Draw a square around the words you don't recognize.

MASTER WORDS

buffet	peremptory
dank	reek
intermittent	savor
mingle	tenant
monologue	visitant

Read the selection on the preceding page again, this time paying special attention to the ten Master Words. In the (a) spaces provided below, write down what you think is the meaning of the word. After you have attempted a definition for each word, look up the word in a dictionary. In the (b) spaces, copy the appropriate dictionary definition.

1. **buffet** (n.)

    a. _____

    b. _____

2. **dank** (adj.)

    a. _____

    b. _____

3. **intermittent** (adj.)

    a. _____

    b. _____

4. **mingle** (v.)

    a. _____

    b. _____

5. **monologue** (n.)

    a. _____

    b. _____

6. **peremptory** (adj.)

    a. _____

    b. _____

7. **reek** (v.)

    a. _____

    b. _____

8. **savor** (n.)

    a. _____

    b. _____

9. **tenant** (n.)

    a. _____

    b. _____

10. **visitant** (n.)

    a. _____

    b. _____

Use the following list of synonyms and antonyms to fill in the blanks. Some words have no antonyms. In such cases, the antonym blanks have been marked with an X.

arid	dialogue	indecisive	renter
blend	flavorlessness	landlord	separate
caress	guest	occupant	soliloquy
commanding	gust	perfume	stink
damp	incessant	periodic	taste

	Synonyms	**Antonyms**
1. **intermittent**	_____	_____
2. **dank**	_____	_____
3. **savor**	_____	_____
4. **mingle**	_____	_____
5. **reek**	_____	_____
6. **buffet**	_____	_____
7. **visitant**	_____	_____
8. **peremptory**	_____	_____
9. **monologue**	_____	_____
10. **tenant**	_____	_____

Decide whether the first pair in the items below are synonyms or antonyms. Then choose the Master Word that shows a similar relation to the word(s) preceding the blank.

1. grotesque	:freakish	::flavor	:	_____
2. garish	:simple	::continual	:	_____
3. resentful	:annoyed	::lodger	:	_____
4. cleave	:separate	::blow	:	_____
5. stress	:strain	::caller	:	_____
6. forbearance	:unrestraint	::dry	:	_____
7. malice	:kindness	::sweeten	:	_____
8. incredible	:likely	::scatter	:	_____
9. potent	:impotent	::wavering	:	_____
10. convulsion	:outburst	::speech	:	_____

LESSON THIRTY-THREE

The Master Words in this lesson are repeated below. From the Master Words, choose the appropriate word for the blank in each of the following sentences. Write the word in the numbered space provided at the right.

buffet	intermittent	monologue	reek	tenant
dank	mingle	peremptory	savor	visitant

1. The priceless wine was kept in (a, an) ...?... underground cave.

1. _____

2. Good ...?...(s) assist in caring for the property they lease.

2. _____

3. First sergeants have a reputation for being ...?... in dealing with recruits who won't "shape up."

3. _____

4. The small car was rudely pitched by ...?...(s) of wind.

4. _____

5. The weatherman changed the forecast from "heavy rain" to "...?... showers."

5. _____

6. They enjoyed the ...?... of the fresh fruit.

6. _____

7. The stand-up comedian's ...?... was filled with political jokes.

7. _____

8. We arrived at the wedding early so we could ...?... with the guests before being seated.

8. _____

9. The house was warmed by the laughter of ...?...(s) who dropped in almost daily.

9. _____

10. The waiting room of the old station seemed to ...?... with the accumulation of a century of smoke.

10. _____

The invented words below are formed from parts of different Master Words from this lesson. Create a definition and indicate the part of speech for each word. The first one is done for you.

buffetmittent   *(adj.) periodically struck by blows* _____

minglonologue   _____

reekermittent   _____

visitenant   _____

Now invent your own words by combining parts of the Master Words. Create a definition for each, and indicate the word's part of speech. (You may reuse any of the word parts above in new combinations.)

1. _____   _____

2. _____   _____

LESSON 34

Read the following selection to get the general meaning. Read it a second time, paying special attention to the words in dark type. Notice how they are used in sentences. These are Master Words. These are the words you will be working with in this lesson.

From **Maggie**
by Stephen Crane

A very little boy stood upon a heap of gravel for the honor of Rum Alley. He was throwing stones at howling **urchins** from Devil's Row who were circling madly about the heap and pelting at him.

His **infantile** countenance was **livid** with fury. His small body was writhing in the delivery of great, crimson oaths.

"Run, Jimmie, run! Dey'll get yehs," screamed a retreating Rum Alley child.

"Naw," responded Jimmie with a **valiant** roar, "dese micks can't make me run."

Howls of renewed wrath went up from Devil's Row throats. Tattered gamins on the right made a furious **assault** on the gravel heap. On their small, convulsed faces there shone the grins of true assassins. As they charged, they threw stones and cursed in shrill chorus.

The little champion of Rum Alley stumbled **precipitately** down the other side. His coat had been torn to shreds in a scuffle, and his hat was gone. He had bruises on twenty parts of his body, and blood was dripping from a cut in his head. His wan features wore a look of a tiny, insane **demon.**

On the ground, children from Devil's Row closed in on their **antagonist.** He **crooked** his left arm defensively about his head and fought with cursing fury. . . .

In the yells of the whirling mob of Devil's Row children there were notes of joy like songs of triumphant savagery. The little boys seemed to leer **gloatingly** at the blood upon the other child's face.

EXERCISE 1

SELF-TEST: After reading the above selection, do the following. Look at the Master Words below. Underline the words that you think you know. Circle the words that you are less sure about. Draw a square around the words you don't recognize.

MASTER WORDS

antagonist	**infantile**
assault	**livid**
crook	**precipitate**
demon	**urchin**
gloat	**valiant**

Read the selection on the preceding page again, this time paying special attention to the ten Master Words. In the (a) spaces provided below, write down what you think is the meaning of the word. After you have attempted a definition for each word, look up the word in a dictionary. In the (b) spaces, copy the appropriate dictionary definition.

1. **antagonist** (n.)

   a. _____

   b. _____

2. **assault** (n.)

   a. _____

   b. _____

3. **crook** (v.)

   a. _____

   b. _____

4. **demon** (n.)

   a. _____

   b. _____

5. **gloat** (v.)

   a. _____

   b. _____

6. **infantile** (adj.)

   a. _____

   b. _____

7. **livid** (adj.)

   a. _____

   b. _____

8. **precipitate** (adj.)

   a. _____

   b. _____

9. **urchin** (n.)

   a. _____

   b. _____

10. **valiant** (adj.)

   a. _____

   b. _____

Use the following list of synonyms and antonyms to fill in the blanks. Some of the words have no antonyms. In such cases, the antonym blanks have been marked with an X.

ally	boast	flushed	imp	straighten
angel	brave	foe	mature	street kid
ashen	cautious	headlong	onslaught	timorous
bend	childish	honor	retreat	

	Synonyms	**Antonyms**
1. **urchin**	_____	_____
2. **demon**	_____	_____
3. **infantile**	_____	_____
4. **antagonist**	_____	_____
5. **livid**	_____	_____
6. **valiant**	_____	_____
7. **assault**	_____	_____
8. **precipitate**	_____	_____
9. **crook**	_____	_____
10. **gloat**	_____	_____

Decide whether the first pair in the items below are synonyms or antonyms. Then choose the Master Word that shows a similar relation to the word(s) preceding the blank.

1. mingle	:sort	::adult	:	_____
2. visitant	:visitor	::brat	:	_____
3. dank	:parched	::partner	:	_____
4. peremptory	:uncertain	::saint	:	_____
5. intermittent	:nonstop	::unbend	:	_____
6. tenant	:roomer	::hurried	:	_____
7. buffet	:blast	::attack	:	_____
8. reek	:stink	::fearless	:	_____
9. monologue	:soliloquy	::brag	:	_____
10. savor	:relish	::colorless	:	_____

The Master Words in this lesson are repeated below. From the Master Words, choose the appropriate word for the blank in each of the following sentences. Write the word in the numbered space provided at the right.

| antagonist | crook | gloat | livid | urchin |
| assault | demon | infantile | precipitate | valiant |

1. It is cheap to ...?... over your triumphs; quiet pride is sufficient after victory.

1._____

2. Pitchers frequently ...?... the elbow and hold the ball on their hips while getting the signs from catchers.

2._____

3. The famous mountain climber knew that one slip would cause (a, an) ...?... plunge down the slope.

3._____

4. The army's ...?... on Pork Chop Hill was accomplished under cover of darkness.

4._____

5. Gothic stories, such as *Dracula*, are not complete without (a, an) ...?... or two.

5._____

6. We would expect such ...?... behavior from someone younger.

6._____

7. The ...?...(s) in *Oliver Twist* deserve sympathy from the reader.

7._____

8. In literature, the character opposing the "hero" is the ...?... .

8._____

9. Our boys made (a, an) ...?... attempt, but the late rally fell short.

9._____

10. The ...?... faces were testimony to the tragedy they had escaped by only inches.

10._____

Order the words in each item from *least* to *most.* Use the abbreviations L for "least" and M for "most." Leave the line before the word of the middle degree blank. The first word provides a clue about how to arrange the words. See the example.

value: ____deficient   L worthless   M satisfactory
(*Worthless* indicates the least value; *satisfactory* indicates the most value.)

1. troublesome:	____rascal	____demon	____angel
2. mature:	____grown-up	____infantile	____adolescent
3. hostile:	____referee	____fan	____antagonist
4. pleased:	____gloat	____scowl	____accept
5. threatening:	____greet	____assault	____challenge
6. pale:	____creamy	____rosy	____livid
7. snarled:	____crook	____tangle	____straighten
8. rushed:	____punctual	____cautious	____precipitate
9. courageous:	____persistent	____timid	____valiant
10. streetwise:	____princess	____urchin	____schoolchild

LESSON **35**

Read the following selection to get the general meaning. Read it a second time, paying special attention to the words in dark type. Notice how they are used in sentences. These are Master Words. These are the words you will be working with in this lesson.

From **"The Haunted and the Haunters"**
by Edward Bulwer-Lytton

We were in the hall, the street-door closed, and my attention was now drawn to my dog. He had at first run in eagerly enough, but had sneaked back to the door, and was scratching and whining to get out. After patting him on the head, and encouraging him gently, the dog seemed to **reconcile** himself to the situation, and followed me through the house, but keeping close at my heels instead of hurrying **inquisitively** in advance, which was his usual and normal habit in all strange places. We first visited the **subterranean** apartments,—the kitchen and other offices, and especially the cellars, in which last there were two or three bottles of wine still left in a bin, covered with cobwebs, and evidently, by their appearance, undisturbed for many years. It was clear that the ghosts were not winebibbers. For the rest we discovered nothing of interest. There was a gloomy little backyard, with very high walls. The stones of this yard were very damp; and what with the damp, and what with the dust and smoke-grime on the pavement, our feet left a slight **impression** where we passed. And now appeared the first strange **phenomenon** witnessed by myself in this strange **abode.** I saw, just before me, the print of a foot suddenly form itself, as it were. I stopped, caught hold of my servant, and pointed to it. In advance of that footprint as suddenly dropped another. We both saw it. I advanced quickly to the place; the footprint kept advancing before me, a small footprint,—the foot of a child: the impression was too faint thoroughly to **distinguish** the shape, but it seemed to us both that it was the print of a naked foot. This phenomenon **ceased** when we arrived at the **opposite** wall, nor did it repeat itself on returning. We remounted the stairs, and entered the rooms on the ground-floor, a dining parlor, a small back-parlor, and a still smaller third room that had been probably **appropriated** to a footman,—all still as death.

EXERCISE 1

SELF-TEST: After reading the above selection, do the following. Look at the Master Words below. Underline the words that you think you know. Circle the words that you are less sure about. Draw a square around the words you don't recognize.

MASTER WORDS

abode	**inquisitive**
appropriate	**opposite**
cease	**phenomenon**
distinguish	**reconcile**
impression	**subterranean**

133

LESSON THIRTY-FIVE

Read the selection on the preceding page again, this time paying special attention to the ten Master Words. In the (a) spaces provided below, write down what you think is the meaning of the word. After you have attempted a definition for each word, look up the word in a dictionary. In the (b) spaces, copy the appropriate dictionary definition.

1. **abode** (n.)

    a. _____

    b. _____

2. **appropriate** (v.)

    a. _____

    b. _____

3. **cease** (v.)

    a. _____

    b. _____

4. **distinguish** (v.)

    a. _____

    b. _____

5. **impression** (n.)

    a. _____

    b. _____

6. **inquisitive** (adj.)

    a. _____

    b. _____

7. **opposite** (adj.)

    a. _____

    b. _____

8. **phenomenon** (n.)

    a. _____

    b. _____

9. **reconcile** (v.)

    a. _____

    b. _____

10. **subterranean** (adj.)

    a. _____

    b. _____

Use the following list of synonyms and antonyms to fill in the blanks. Some words have no antonyms. In such cases, the antonym blanks have been marked with an X.

aerial	continue	elevation	supposition
alienate	contrary	happening	terminate
allot	curious	homelessness	underground
conciliate	discriminate	imprint	uninterested
confuse	dwelling	similar	withhold

	Synonyms	**Antonyms**
1. **reconcile**	_____	_____
2. **inquisitive**	_____	_____
3. **subterranean**	_____	_____
4. **distinguish**	_____	_____
5. **impression**	_____	_____
6. **phenomenon**	_____	_____
7. **abode**	_____	_____
8. **cease**	_____	_____
9. **opposite**	_____	_____
10. **appropriate**	_____	_____

EXERCISE 4 ▬▬▬▬▬▬▬▬▬▬▬▬▬▬▬▬▬▬▬▬▬▬▬▬

Decide whether the first pair in the items below are synonyms or antonyms. Then choose the Master Word that shows a similar relation to the word(s) preceding the blank.

1. infantile	:developed	::unconcerned	: _____
2. crook	:uncurl	::overlook	: _____
3. gloat	:triumph	::assign	: _____
4. urchin	:ragamuffin	::buried	: _____
5. livid	:pale	::mark	: _____
6. assault	:raid	::home	: _____
7. precipitate	:abrupt	::event	: _____
8. demon	:angel	::same	: _____
9. valiant	:afraid	::separate	: _____
10. antagonist	:comrade	::proceed	: _____

The Master Words in this lesson are repeated below. From the Master Words, choose the appropriate word for the blank in each of the following sentences. Write the word in the numbered space provided at the right.

abode	cease	impression	opposite	reconcile
appropriate	distinguish	inquisitive	phenomenon	subterranean

1. Below London is (a, an) ...?... network of pulsing transportation known as "the tube."

1. _____

2. Lightning is one ...?... of nature.

2. _____

3. Flowers are (a, an) ...?... gift for both males and females.

3. _____

4. Perhaps we can ...?... our differences and get together again.

4. _____

5. Most people believe that Democrats and Republicans are ...?... in principle.

5. _____

6. The rain should ...?... by midnight and be followed by a cold wave.

6. _____

7. The ...?... of a single footprint in the sand is Robinson Crusoe's first introduction to Friday.

7. _____

8. We could not ...?... the original painting from its reproduction.

8. _____

9. (A, an) ...?... child is likely to ask questions.

9. _____

10. The robin's winter ...?... is the more sunny regions of the south.

10. _____

EXERCISE 6 ■■

To complete the crossword, choose the Master Word associated with each word or phrase below. Begin each answer in the square having the same number as the clue.

1. can be a cottage or castle

2. bring together feuding friends

3. Sherlock Holmes was this

4. the other side of the coin

5. *Journey to the Center of the Earth*

6. tell red from green or soft from loud

7. what Congress does to funds

8. put a halt to

9. track in the mud

10. can be an everyday event or an eye-opener

LESSON 36 Review of Lessons 25–35

PART I: From the list below, choose the correct word for each sentence that follows. Use each word only once.

antagonist	illumination	interminable	tenant
dank	induce	persistence	transgression
fugitive	inquisitive	puny	valiant

1. The basement was so musty and _____ that the owner decided to buy a dehumidifier.

2. The boy was so _____ that he seemed too weak even to be the waterboy.

3. Their _____ efforts to sandbag the riverbanks prevented flooding.

4. The candles produced so much _____ that they did not need to turn the lights on.

5. His _____, evidenced by long hours of extra practice, finally won him a position on the first string.

6. The car ads try to _____ reluctant buyers to take a test drive.

7. The desperate _____ knew he must cover his trail or he would be caught and returned to prison.

8. The week before summer vacation seems _____ to an anxious youngster.

9. The landlord had to evict the noisy _____.

10. Because of his _____ nature, Danny was constantly asking questions.

11. The unfair tactics of the _____ nearly spelled defeat for the hero.

12. Because Tom's _____ hurt the whole family, his parents punished him.

PART II: From the list below, choose the correct word for each sentence that follows. Use each word only once.

annihilate	garish	inexplicable	sturdy
circuitous	grimace	intermittent	subterranean
endure	indignation	remote	yield

1. The _____ rain alternately raised and lowered the hopes of the picnickers.

2. True pioneers _____ great hardships but seldom give up their struggle.

3. The rabbits scampered to their _____ hiding places, where the hunters could not reach them.

4. Because Lorraine failed to _____ at the intersection, she was stopped by an officer.

5. When Brent saw Carolyn _____ with displeasure, he knew she disliked the painting.

6. The dress was so tasteless and _____ that the store couldn't sell it.

7. The angry executive bridled with _____ when he was accused of bribing foreign officials.

8. The shoes were advertised as being _____, but they started to come apart almost immediately.

9. Cut off from their supplies, the battalion will be _____(d, ed) unless air support is called in.

10. The path cut such (a, an) _____ route through the woods that the trail resembled a maze.

11. The cause of the man's death remained _____ even after the autopsy.

12. Although the village is quite _____ and thus hard to reach, many tourists visit it each year.

PART III: Decide whether the first pair in the items below are synonyms or antonyms. Then choose the Master Word from Lessons 25-35 which shows a similar relation to the word(s) preceding the blank. Do not repeat a Master Word that appears in the first column.

1. crook	:curve	::guarantee	: _____
2. keen	:excited	::settle	: _____
3. insolent	:courteous	::charity	: _____
4. provocation	:annoyance	::almighty	: _____
5. yield	:surrender	::polite	: _____
6. deride	:value	::adult	: _____
7. valiant	:cowardly	::uninterrupted	: _____
8. grotesque	:attractive	::pass by	: _____
9. mingle	:mix	::sin	: _____
10. affability	:agreeableness	::liveliness	: _____
11. wax	:enlarge	::unthinkable	: _____
12. vortex	:stillness	::by hand	: _____
13. livid	:blushing	::commonplace	: _____
14. inquisitive	:questioning	::heavy	: _____
15. malice	:ill will	::dare	: _____
16. propound	:hold back	::slow	: _____
17. preside	:chair	::anger	: _____
18. ostensibly	:seemingly	::suitably	: _____
19. convulsion	:tranquillity	::degenerate	: _____
20. corroborate	:contradict	::pullout	: _____

INDEX—Word and Lesson Number